# The Wild Side

## *Volume 2*

SCOTT SHALAWAY

SADDLE RIDGE PRESS
CAMERON, WEST VIRGINIA

# TABLE OF CONTENTS

## Part 2.   Purely Personal

## Part 3.   Adventure/Travel

## Part 4.  Backyard Wildlife

10-5-97

## For More Information

# Acknowledgements

Thanks to all who read my column, especially those who take time to write with questions, encouragement and criticism.  You are truly the reason I have been able to write his column for ten years and counting.

Thanks to every newspaper editor who has given my column a forum.  Competition for space is always keen, so I appreciate your support and confidence.

And to my wife, Linda, and my daughters, Nora and Emma, thanks for tolerating the odd hours I sometimes keep, the roadkills in the yard and the dead stuff in the freezer.

# Preface

Though the first collection of my newspaper columns entitled *The Wild Side* is out of print, I continue to get requests for copies. Rather than reprint the original book, I've compiled a new volume of more recent material. Most originally appeared in my syndicated newspaper column, though a few of the longer pieces are reprints of magazine articles. The "hole" story and the hummingbird questions and answers also appeared in my book *BIRDS, Bats, Butterflies... and Other Backyard Beasts*.

I've organized this book into four sections -- natural history, personal perspectives, travel/adventure and backyard tips for wildlife watchers. The date that accompanies each piece indicates the month and year it first appeared in print.

Whether you aggressively manage your backyard to attract wildlife or prefer the more passive approach of enjoying nature from an easy chair, I hope you will find this book entertaining, informative and perhaps even insightful.

Another reason I compile these columns into books is to create a personal history for my daughters. Twenty years from now, they will have a better idea of what I did and where I was when they were in school.

One final note of explanation. You will quickly discover that there are no illustrations in this book. That was a conscious decision on my part. Drawings and photographs add to the cost of production. In order to keep the price of the book reasonable at a time when paper prices are at record highs, I elected to forgo illustrations. I hope you approve.

Scott Shalaway
Marshall County, West Virginia
10 October 1996

*to the memories of Aldo Leopold and Roger Tory Peterson*

# Part 1

# Natural History

I like back roads. Back roads often follow streams, which attract wildlife... and wildlife watchers.

A kingfisher hovering, then diving for a meal, or a brood of wood ducks dutifully following their mom -- sights such as these are sure to send my foot to the brake.

If I'm especially attentive, I sometimes spot a stately great blue heron fishing along the shore. Even at 40 miles per hour on a winding country road, sudden movements can catch the eye. The heron's long neck fires and recoils, stabbing the surface of the quiet pool. I slam on the brakes just in time to watch the stately great blue flip a minnow into the air and swallow it whole.

Found along virtually every waterway in North America, great blues often escape detection despite their five-ft. tall profile. Usually they stand quietly in the shallows scanning the water for fish. As fish approach, the heron freezes. When a fish swims within reach, the long powerful neck explodes to full extension. In literally a blink of an eye the strike is complete.

Great blues grab small fish crosswise in their bill then lift their heads and finesse the fish until it can be swallowed headfirst. Larger fish, likewise, are swallowed headfirst, but are caught by spearing with the long pointed bill.

Despite its impressive size, a great blue heron can be difficult to spot. It can stand motionless for long periods of time, so our eyes often miss it. Only when we glimpse a sudden movement along a lake shore or stream bank do we notice its presence.

More often we see one flying overhead. The seven-ft. wingspan, slow wing beats, neck drawn back in an "S" curve and long legs trailing behind the body make great blue herons easy to recognize. The blue-gray body and black and white neck and head are usually lost in silhouette.

Many people see these tall, long-legged birds and call them cranes or storks. In fact, I get calls to that effect several times each year. But cranes and storks rarely visit here.

In parts of the country where both cranes and storks live, however, there's an easy way to tell them apart. Cranes and storks fly with their necks extended. Herons (and egrets, for that matter) fly with their necks pulled back in an "S' shaped position.

Just a few minutes spent watching a heron hunt teaches any patient observer that many strikes are unsuccessful. Like any other frustrated fisherman, a great blue will eventually move to another spot.

A heron's hunting success ranges from 25 to 50 percent. That may not seem too impressive at first. But consider that a baseball player who gets a hit 30 percent of the time is Hall of Fame material. Or ask any angler. If he (or she) caught a fish every three or four casts, you couldn't drag him off the water.

Despite the great blue's attraction to water, its diet is not limited to fish. It also eats frogs, snakes, crayfish, insects, shrimp, crabs and even mice, shrews, and small rats. The varied diet may make feeding young herons a bit more manageable, especially in dry years.

Unlike many birds, great blue herons are communal nesters -- they nest in colonies. These nesting rookeries, as they are called, often include nests of several species of wading birds. Both parents take turns incubating the four or five eggs for about 28 days during late spring. Newly hatched young remain in the nest for two to three months before fledging.

An active rookery can get crowded and noisy. Each tree may hold several nests and a dozen or more young birds. Fortunately, rookeries are usually in remote woodlands where detection by humans is unlikely.

Great blue herons linger in the area well into the fall -- as long as there's ice-free water for fishing. During mild winters they sometimes stay all year.

Next time you drive along a stream or river or skirt a lake, keep your eyes peeled for sudden movement. You'll be in great blue country.

The golden harvest moon hung low on the horizon as a pair of flying squirrels left their den for their early evening meal. The woods had been generous this year. Oaks and hickories hung heavy with mast and just as many nuts had already fallen to the ground. The flying squirrels had never known such bounty. Perhaps that's why they let their vigilance slip.

Fifty yards away a Great Horned Owl perched in a tall cherry tree and watched patiently. Without a sound, the owl dropped into the air and sailed silently toward the gluttonous flying squirrels. At the last instant, the squirrels sensed disaster and leaped into the air. The flaps of skin that run from their wrists to their ankles filled with air and the squirrels glided toward the safety of their den tree.

One had a split second head start. It landed on the trunk and instantly scooted to the opposite side of the tree. This little maneuver insures that winged pursuers grab only bark.

The owl, however, had wisely zeroed in on the other squirrel. With safety just seconds away, the squirrel could feel the "whoosh" of the owl's silent flight. Eight needle-sharp talons impaled the squirrel's body. Death followed quickly, and the great horned owl filled its crop.

Near a barn on the edge of the wood's a half mile away, another deadly drama unfolded. In this case, however, the victim was a juvenile cat, and the predator was the first owl's mate. The cat was also hunting -- mice, voles or roosting birds. The owl launched its attack from its perch on a power line pole. The hunter became the hunted.

It was a good evening. The pair went two for two.

East of the Mississippi River, where wolves and mountain lions were exterminated decades ago, where black bears roam only certain mountainous areas, where bobcats are so secretive their presence goes almost unnoticed, the great horned owl reigns as king of the woods.

I give great horned owls this title because they sit atop the food chain. They eat everything from insects to crows, bats, squirrels, skunks, raccoons, porcupines, weasels and other owls, though mice, rats and rabbits comprise most of their diet. Great horned owls are even known to take turkeys off the roost and new born fawns.

When food is abundant, great horns sometimes kill much more than they need and eat only the best parts. When food is scarce, they cache store their kills and return repeatedly until the carcass is picked clean. During very cold weather these stored kills can freeze. Great horns solve this problem quite simply. They incubate the frozen prey until it thaws. Then they eat it.

Rarely, however, does anything eat an adult great horned owl. Crows may occasionally grab eggs or small chicks at an unprotected nest, but most horned owl mortality can be attributed to disease, accidental death and ignorant fools with nothing better to do than shoot protected birds.

Despite their size -- two feet tall and a wingspan of up to five feet -- great horned owls often go undetected in the woods. They spend their days perched quietly in conifers or in deciduous trees that cling tenaciously to clumps of dead leaves. And they spread themselves out. A single bird may cover more than a square mile in the course of its daily activities. So your chances of seeing one on a walk in the woods are slim.

The best time to find great horned owls is in late November and December. This is when males and females court and call. Great horned owls are the "hoot owl" so many people hear, but seldom see. Listen for a series of three to seven simple hoots. A five-syllable call may suggest the phrase, "Don't kill owls, save owls!"

When you hear a call, follow it into the woods. Tread lightly and quietly until the serenade gets louder. If you're lucky you spot an owl perched high on a horizontal branch close to the tree trunk. Or you may glimpse a large ghostly form swoop through the woods.

An easier way to find owls is to follow crows and jays. When corvids spot a roosting owl, they just can't help themselves. They sound the alarm and in just minutes a mob scene ensues. Angry corvids send a clear message: "We've spotted you. We're going to harass you until you leave. So beat it!" It usually takes a few minutes for the owl to get the message, so if you reach the scene quickly, you can often spot the owl.

Over a period of weeks in December and January, the male woos the female. He feeds her. He performs noisy aerial displays. He defends her. Eventually they get serious and

4

select a nest.    Great horned owls don't build their own nests; they take over someone else's.   Often it's an old red-tailed hawk  or squirrel nest, but occasionally they occupy a large tree cavity or even an extra large nest box.   If the female is experienced,  she usually uses the same nest she used the last year.

The female lays the first of her two or three eggs in late January or early February.   Three days later she lays another. If food is abundant, she may lay a third egg, but as often as not, two eggs complete the clutch.   Though the eggs are laid at three-day intervals, incubation begins immediately with the first egg.   This is why you may see photographs of owlets of several sizes in the same nest.   The eldest sibling in a brood of three may be six days older than the youngest.

Incubation continues for 26 to 35 days; the first egg laid is the first to hatch.   Because great horned owls nest so early, the nest often gets covered with a blanket of snow.   It seems a harsh way to bring a brood into the world, but the parents don't seem to mind.   They take turns warming the eggs. Snow may blanket the incubating parent, but its soft downy feathers keep the eggs warm and dry.

Nestling horned owls grow rapidly and quickly develop the ability to regulate their own body temperature, but they remain in the nest for more than two months.   They begin to exercise their wings at six weeks, but cannot fly until they are about 10 weeks old.   Young owls perfect their hunting skills slowly and remain dependent on their parents for food well into fall.

Learning the skills to hunt successfully takes time and practice, but once mastered, nothing in the woods does it better than the great horned owl.

When I moved to my ridge-top home in northern West Virginia, I expected to hear whip-poor-wills during spring migration. I even hoped a few would stay to nest.

As one of those considerate birds that sings its own name, or that was named for its song (depending on your point of view), the whip-poor-will is easy to recognize by sound. Over and over, sometimes for minutes at a time, males advertise their presence to attract a mate.

I first learned the song of the whip-poor-will at a friend's house in the woods of northeastern Oklahoma. There, at the western edge of the eastern deciduous forest, a chorus of whip-poor-wills and chuck-wills-widows ushered in each summer eve. Though their songs are quite similar, whip's song consists of three notes, while chuck sings four. Even kids quickly learn the difference. The serenade began a few minutes after sunset and continued for hours.

My first seven years here on the ridge, however, were disappointing. The music of the night that echoes through my woods is rich in owls, frogs and insects, but I've missed the whip-poor-will. Evenings are rarely quiet, but they always sound incomplete. I felt cheated by the whip-poor-will's absence.

Until May 1991.

I sat on the deck with Emma, who was not quite three, watching darkness claim the remains of the day. A robin squawked as it settled in to roost, spring peepers echoed in the hollow below and a final wood thrush chorus drifted up from the hollow. As the sky grew black, stars began to twinkle.

Then, in the distance, I heard three faint, familiar notes. "Whip-poor-will." And again, "Whip-poor-will." For a full minute the bird sang. I smiled. The song was too soft, the bird too distant, to try to point it out to Emma. I waited.

After a few minutes of silence, the bird called again. It had moved closer to the house, so now the song was much louder. Emma heard it and sensed my excitement. She listened carefully. Then again the bird fell silent.

Though often heard, whip-poor-wills are seldom seen. They spend the daylight hours nestled on the forest floor, where their drably colored bodies blend in perfectly with the forest floor, or perched lengthwise overhead on a horizontal branch. Whip-poor-wills usually sit tightly, confident in their camouflage. When danger approaches too closely, however, they flush and fly away silently like giant moths.

At dusk whip-poor-wills come to life, venture to woodland clearings, and earn their living by snatching moths, beetles and other night flying insects. Their huge gaping mouths, surrounded by a ring of specialized feathers called rictal bristles, become efficient aerial nets perfectly designed for capturing flying insects.

After dark, whip-poor-wills may be seen along wooded, country roads. Watch for their distinctive red eye shine as they bathe in the dust along the roadside.

Whip-poor-will don't waste much energy while nesting. The female lays two mottled eggs directly on the forest floor; there is no nest. She incubates the eggs alone for about 20 days, and just 20 days later the young whip-poor-wills can fly and begin to learn to fend for themselves.

Suddenly, the whip-poor-will called again. He had come even closer -- to the edge of the yard. Emma heard it clearly and began mimicking, "Whip-poor-will, whip-poor-will."

Then we witnessed what I call a "wild moment" -- a close encounter with nature that stays with you forever. As I gazed in the direction of the song, a dark form came gliding from the woods directly toward the deck. It cruised in just four feet above the ground, heading straight for the house.

Apparently the whip-poor-will was attracted to the insects hovering near the deck light. As it reached the edge of the deck, it pulled up, snatched a moth from the air, turned and flew back into the woods. When it turned, large white patches on its fanned tail confirmed that the bird was a male.

Several minutes later, he called again. By now it was completely dark, and my wife, Linda, and eight-year old Nora had joined us on the deck. We listened for 20 more minutes, so Emma and Nora could tune their ears to this special music of the night.

Hearing whip-poor-wills has not always been so unusual. But like many forest birds, their numbers have been in a tailspin for more than 20 years. The *Atlas of Breeding Birds in Pennsylvania* reports, "This species, formerly a characteristic night bird across Pennsylvania, is now greatly reduced in numbers and distribution." It occurred in only 17 percent of the survey blocks across the state.

Because the song of the whip-poor-will is so familiar, especially to older folks who grew up in rural areas, I'm frequently asked, "Where have all the whip-poor-wills gone?" That's a good question to which there is no single correct answer. Their decline is probably due to a combination of factors.

Whip-poor-wills eat flying insects, so their reproductive rate may have dipped in the 1940s, 50s and 60s as the use of toxic pesticides peaked. A population decline could be attributed to either a declining food supply or indirect poisoning from eating contaminated prey.

Because they require woodlands interspersed with clearings, perhaps Pennsylvania's maturing forests are getting too old for whip-poor-wills. As openings disappear, whip-poor-wills are squeezed out.

Another likely culprit is forest fragmentation. Though small chunks of forest may provide excellent habitat for whip-poor-wills, populations of blue jays, crows, grackles, feral cats and raccoons also increase in these areas. Heavy nest predation decimates breeding populations of forest song birds; so these abundant predators probably take a toll on whip-poor-wills, too.

And of course, because whip-poor-wills migrate, there may be problems on their wintering grounds. Given so many strikes against them, it's a wonder we see any whip-poor-wills at all.

I must add that not everyone shares my affection and enthusiasm for these vocal night birds. One neighbor in particular has complained that whip-poor-wills keep him up all night. It seems every night, May through July, an ardent male sings from a pine tree just outside his bedroom window. The serenade begins at dusk, continues late into the evening, and then resumes several hours before dawn. I've reminded him that one man's trash is another's treasure, but he failed to get the point or the humor. However, when I explained the bird's plight, he said he'd try earplugs.

In ten years, I've heard a whip-poor-will just once. Perhaps that's why it means so much. Rarity confers value. When I went to bed that night, the cry of the whip-poor-will lulled me to sleep. It was a night I'll never forget. It was the night of the whip-poor-will.

As he tells it, my neighbor had been sitting comfortably in his tree stand for several hours. His eyes grew heavy, and soon he fell asleep. Moments later he roused to a series of loud staccato shrieks. He opened his eyes and saw a large black and white bird flying straight at him.

In those few seconds of semi-consciousness between sleep and wakefulness, he felt panic, fear, even terror, not knowing if the "attack" was real, imagined or dream-induced.

But almost immediately he realized that he was awake, and the intruder was simply curious. He kept his camo-clothed body motionless, and the "Indian hen," as he called it, landed right next to him. It examined him for several seconds, knowing that this lump was not a part of the normal landscape. Finally, satisfied that the foreign object represented no threat, the bird flew off, cackling again like a tropical jungle bird.

Based on my friend's enthusiastic telling of the encounter, he was more excited by the close encounter than embarrassed by having fallen asleep in his stand. And I don't blame him. It's not every day a pileated woodpecker lands within arm's reach.

Pileated (PIE-lee-ated is the preferred pronunciation, PIL-ee-ated is acceptable) woodpeckers are crested, crow-sized, black, white and red woodpeckers that inhabit mature eastern forests. Because they are big birds, they require big trees in which to excavate their nest and roost cavities. That's why they seek mature forests. Young timber stands simply don't have trees large enough to meet their needs.

Older stands also provide the proper winter diet. During cold weather, pileateds eat large black carpenter ants that inhabit dead and decaying branches, logs and stumps. These ants are what pileateds are hunting when they visit an old stump and appear to tear it apart. Younger forest stands lack large pieces of dead wood and the ants that inhabit it.

This magnificent "crested woodcutter" (the literal translation of its scientific name, *Dryocopus pileatus*) is truly a sight to behold. But pileateds are more often heard than seen. So jungle-like are their loud "cuk, cuk, cuk" calls that they remind me of an old Tarzan movie. And their habit of drumming on resonant dead branches also attracts immediate attention. Both sounds carry far through the woods and help mated pairs communicate. These sounds also declare ownership of a territory that may exceed 200 acres.

Courtship is in full swing right now. I hear calls and drumming every morning. Though pileateds pair for life, these behaviors strengthen the bonds for the upcoming nesting season. The pair works together to excavate a new nest cavity that will soon cradle a clutch of four white eggs. The three and one-half inch hole opens into a cavity that may be as much as two feet deep.

Incubation lasts 16 to 18 days, and unlike many birds, the male does more than his fair share. During the day the parents take turns incubating in one or two hour stretches, but the male warms the eggs at night. The female sleeps in a nearby roosting cavity.

After the eggs hatch, the parents spend the next month feeding the hungry growing brood. But even if you watch a nest closely, it's difficult to know when hatching occurs. The adults feed the chicks by regurgitation, so you're unlikely to see an adult carry food to the nest. When the chicks are about two weeks old, they begin to climb to the hole to wait for the next feeding.

Finding an active pileated cavity is not as difficult as it may seem. Hike through portions of the woods where you hear pileateds and search the ground for piles of fresh wood chips. Twenty to 80 feet directly above, you should find a hole.

## *Chickadees* (1/94)

Mid-winter's a real beast for creatures that contend with it on a daily basis -- especially small birds such as chickadees. One major cost of small size is rapid heat loss. That's why small animals tend to have higher metabolic rates than larger ones.

So how do small birds manage to eat enough food each day to survive 14-hour winter nights? Most birds that visit feeders do it by eating oily, energy rich seeds. Sunflower, safflower and thistle seeds are high in fat, so finches and other seed-eaters easily acquire enough fat each day to make it through the night.

But how about chickadees? Though common backyard birds, research indicates chickadees that visit backyard feeders get only about 25 percent of their daily diet at feeders. The rest consists of insect egg cases, larvae and pupae they find hidden in bark crevices or under loose bark.

Weighing in at just 10 to 12 grams -- about a third of an ounce -- chickadees are common throughout the U.S. How can such tiny birds possibly make it through the winter on a high protein, low fat diet? The answer is the fascinating story of how one species has adapted to a hostile, seasonal environment.

The chickadee's challenge is finding enough food during winter's short days to survive long winter nights. Actually, eastern chickadees have it easy; in Alaska Black-capped Chickadees get barely 3.5 hours of daylight at winter solstice. But geography aside, winter's challenge remains.

Chickadees cope with severe weather and long cold nights in three ways: physically, physiologically and behaviorally.

Physically, they combat the worst of winter with a dense insulating coat of feathers. At the end of the summer, chickadees molt -- they grow a new set of feathers. Therefore they enter fall and winter with the best insulation nature can provide. By spring, wear and feather loss have greatly reduced the insulating ability of the feather mass.

Many animals, especially mammals, take the physiological route to protect themselves from winter cold. Some add layers of body fat. Chickadees do too, but each night they burn all the fat they stored the day before. So chickadees can't rely on fat to insulate their body cores. They do, however, use it to fuel their metabolic furnaces to get them through the night. Each day chickadees double their early morning fat reserves. That fat then burns off during the night.

Chickadees make most efficient use of their daily fat stores by reducing their metabolic needs to match the amount of energy available. They cannot consume enough food each day to maintain their normal body temperature of 42°C (107.6° F). Instead, on cold nights, chickadees enter a controlled state of hypothermia. Their body temperature drops 10 to 12 °C below the day time temperature of 42° C. When the air temperature is 0°C (32° F), chickadees can reduce their metabolic costs by as much as 23 percent. Consequently chickadees make it through the night on about half the calories they'd need if they did not become hypothermic. Thus, they survive on a high protein, low fat winter diet.

Chickadees also counter winter cold with a variety of adaptive behaviors. For example, they escape wind, rain, sleet and snow by sleeping in dense vegetation such as conifers or small cavities. When cavities are used, they are much smaller than a nesting cavity. In fact, they are usually just big enough for the chickadee to get inside. The empty space in such small cavities is quickly warmed by heat loss from the bird, and the cavity becomes a cozy little bedroom. In such small cavities total radiant and convection heat loss is reduced 60 to 100 percent. Though not as effective as cavities, dense evergreen vegetation also offers protection from the elements.

Chickadees enhance the protective value of a roost further simply by adjusting their posture. They fluff their feathers to cover their naked legs and feet, and they tuck their beak and part of their face into the shoulder feathers on the wing. This posture reduces the heat loss from unfeathered parts of the body.

Another simple way that chickadees change their behavior to reduce their energy needs is to slow down. On cold windy days, they fly less frequently, they move less often from place to place, and spend more time at any given food source. You can observe this at your own feeders. Compare how long chickadees stay at feeders on cold, windy days to their visits on calm, mild days.

On windy days chickadees avoid foraging in the treetops. Instead they spend more time close to the tree trunks and closer to the ground. That's because wind speed is slower closer to the ground, thanks to dense ground level vegetation. In effect, chickadees reduce the effects of the wind-chill factor by avoiding high winds.

The greatest danger that chickadees face in winter are the periodic blizzards and ice storms that lock away foods and can quickly lead to starvation. That's where their food storing skill comes in handy. Throughout the fall and into early winter, chickadees scatter small caches of food throughout their winter range. Those that roost in cavities store food there, too. Thus during winter storms chickadees have a safety net of stored food that can see them through a stressful day or two until natural foods become available.

Despite their small size and fragile appearance, chickadees cope remarkably well with severe winter weather. Thanks to dense plumage, nightly hypothermia and a variety of adaptive behaviors, chickadees thrive when most other creatures either hibernate or migrate.

## *Nuthatches* (12/86)

When I want to think or just need to get away from the chaos of everyday life, I head for the woods. I have a favorite spot on some moss-covered rocks that overlook a small stream flowing 100 feet below. The peace and quiet of the forest never fail to work their magic.

Invariably, however, one of my favorite woodland birds breaks my concentration. Even with my eyes closed, its nasal, "Ank, ank, ank" call alerts me to the presence of a white-breasted nuthatch. I don't wish to be rude so I open my eyes and scan the treetops. It doesn't take long to spot the blue-gray acrobat.

I see it first as it works its way head-first down the trunk of a large white oak tree. Quickly flitting to a nearby branch, it hangs upside-down and nabs a cold, groggy spider. In jerky, almost mechanical movements, it continues up and down the tree. I flatter myself by thinking the performance is just for me.

Nuthatches are most visible during fall and winter. On leafless trees, they are easily spotted as they work their way down and around the tree trunks.

They are small, handsome birds. Only five inches long, they have a white breast and face with a blue-gray back and a black cap and neck. Females resemble males, but are duller. Their acrobatic, upside down antics, however, are the best clue to their identity.

Nuthatches regularly visit backyard feeders, but they don't travel in feeding flocks like chickadees, titmice and goldfinches. A single pair works my yard each morning. And even when I can't see the birds, I can hear them "anking" in the distance.

Adults maintain a loose pair bond even during the winter months. Often they travel alone, but within earshot of each other. Their winter feeding territory measures 25 to 50 acres. At night each roosts alone in its own tree cavity. Come May, the female finds a new cavity in which to build a nest and lay her eggs.

Voracious insect predators during warmer weather, nuthatches turn to nuts and seeds in fall and winter. After working their way down a tree trunk, they frequently search the ground for fallen acorns, beechnuts and hickory nuts. Perhaps that's why they look so natural combing the ground under feeders for fallen sunflower seeds.

The nuthatch uses an ingenious technique it uses to open acorns and other nuts. Lacking a seed-cracking bill, it wedges a nut into a crevice in a piece of bark and hammers with its bill until the shell breaks. No mean feat, especially with a hickory nut. They use the same technique to open sunflower seeds at the feeder.

Like blue jays and red-bellied woodpeckers, nuthatches cache nuts and seeds for times when food might be in short supply. It is difficult to determine what portion of their food they eat and how much is stashed in small tree cavities or under loose slabs of bark.

Nuthatches also eat suet. Whether taken from a carcass in the woods or from a feeder in the yard, animal fat provides valuable energy on cold winter nights. Nuthatches often demonstrate their acrobatic skills by hanging upside-down from the suet basket as they feed.

White-breasted nuthatches live all year in oak-hickory forests, wooded parks and backyards. Watch for them in any wooded neighborhood. And don't be surprised to see its equally acrobatic four-inch cousin, the red-breasted nuthatch, a winter visitor from farther north. Red-breasts nest in northern coniferous forests and venture south in the fall to open deciduous woods and backyards, where they, too, eat sunflower seeds and suet. They can be distinguished from white-breasted nuthatches by their smaller size, rusty bellies and a striking black eyeline topped by a white eyebrow stripe.

If you spot an unfamiliar acrobat at your feeders this winter, chances are you're watching a nuthatch. You'll quickly discover it's one of your backyard's friendliest and most fascinating visitors.

## *A Bluebird Diary* (3/93)

The story of nest box HM-4 began in February when I strapped it to a fence post on a neighbor's farm. This box was one of four that I hung along the fence that enclosed a large pasture. By getting the boxes up in the middle of winter, they would become a part of the landscape and be more likely to be used later on.

I first noticed bluebirds investigating HM-4 in early March. As I paralleled the fence on my way to town, I saw a female fly from the box. I stopped the car and watched. Moments later, the male lighted on the box. Then the female returned and entered the box. Then the male joined her inside. After about a minute the male emerged and once again perched on the roof of the box. He watched as his mate flew to a nearby tree. This curious investigation of the box continued for the entire 30 minutes I watched. Clearly the bluebirds were considering HM-4 as a nest site.

Ideally a bluebird box should be hung about four feet above the ground. It should be at least 50 yards from the nearest wooded area, though it's OK if there are a few scattered trees nearby. And to minimize competitive squabbling with neighboring bluebirds, the next nearest nest box should be no closer than 100 yards. At least that's an ornithologist's prescription for a successful nest box. HM-4 met all these requirements. Now I'd have a chance to see if these birds did "what they were supposed to do."

For the next two weeks, I saw the bluebirds every time I drove past the box. Sometimes they were on it as before. Other time they were nearby hawking insects from a nearby snag or eating rose hips in a nearby multiflora rose thicket. So far so good. What follows is a "diary" of events that I observed at HM-4.

**March 17**. HM-4 contained a completed bluebird nest. It was made entirely of dried grasses and filled the box almost to the hole. The cup itself was lined with fine grasses, while the foundation consisted of courser material. The bluebirds had committed to the box.

**March 24**. No change. The female had not yet begun laying eggs.

**March 29**. Two sky blue eggs rested in the nest. The adults were nowhere to be found. During the egg-laying period, the female visits the nest only early in the morning to lay that day's egg. This reduces the chances that a predator will see her near the nest and gives her time to feed in anticipation to the family commitment she is about to make.

**April 1**. As I drive by the box, the female leaves so I stop to check the box. Since the female's already gone, I know I'll not disturb her. The nest now contains five eggs and they are warm to my touch. The clutch is complete and the 14-day incubation period has begun. I note the date so I won't disturb the nest again until just a few days before hatching. Incubating females are sensitive to disturbance during the first half of the incubation period and may abandon the nest if disturbed during this time.

**April 4**. A late winter storm dumps 16 inches of wet, heavy snow on the area. I wonder how the bluebirds are faring, but resist the temptation to check on them.

**April 11**. I approach the box quietly on foot, hoping to catch the female on the nest so I can band her. Late in incubation (this is the 11th of 14 days), females sit tight. Their investment in the nest has reached a critical stage and they flee only if seriously threatened. I place one hand over the hole and slide the other under the door, on top of the incubating female. I grab her firmly and band, weigh and measure her. The entire process takes less than 60 seconds. Then I put her back on her five eggs, close the door and hold my hand over the hole for about a minute to be sure she's settled down. I walk away and she remains on the nest as if she was never disturbed.

**April 14.** Right on schedule, four tiny hatchlings occupy the nest. The fifth egg is pipped and ready to hatch. Mom sits on the barbed wire fences and scolds me from just six feet away. Dad buzzes my head. I take the hint and leave. Within two minutes of my departure, the female resumes brooding the chicks.

**April 16.** I park my car about 50 feet from the box and watch. About every three minutes one of the parents visits the nest with a meal for the kids. Grubs and soft fleshy caterpillars seem the food of choice. In another week the chicks will be eating grasshoppers and other harder bodied insects.

**April 26.** The chicks are now 12 days old and ready to be banded. Perhaps some of them will use one of my boxes next year.

**April 29.** The chicks now fill the box and whitewash covers the walls. They will fledge in a few days so this will be my last visit to the box. Disturbing a box after chicks are 15 days old may cause them to fledge before they can fly, making them easy prey for snakes, cats, raccoons and other predators.

**May 2.** I notice several speckled juvenile bluebirds in the oak tree near HM-4. With my binoculars I can see their bands, and after scanning the branches I count a total of five. Success!

Bluebirds raise two or three broods each year, so I remove the old soiled nest to be sure the box is free of debris and parasites before the next nest.

Nothing in nature gives me more satisfaction than watching a pair of birds raise a brood in a nest box I've provided because I know that without my help they may not have nested. It personalizes conservation.

HM-4 proved especially rewarding because the same pair of bluebirds raised two more broods in it that summer. The last fledged in late August. That more than made up for some of my other boxes the birds ignored.

(The easiest way to become an active conservationist is to build nest boxes. It makes an especially great project for youth groups. Depending on the size of the box and where it's placed, tenants may include bluebirds, chickadees, titmice, nuthatches, wrens, tree swallows, great-crested flycatchers, screech-owls, kestrels and wood ducks.)

*same -* **Cardinals** (3/94)

It's a sight you never forget: a flock of bright red male cardinals perched in a drab, leafless tree on a snowy winter day. Their very presence brightens the day and lifts the spirit.

In the spring the male's song tells us warmer days lie just ahead. "What cheer! What cheer! What cheer!" or "Purdy, purdy, purdy," are just two of the familiar songs that let us identify cardinals by sound.

In the summer, after raising a brood or two, parent cardinals escort their family to backyard feeding stations. The elders introduce the young to their favorite fast food -- sunflower seeds.

Finally, in the fall, family groups come together to form the flocks that later in the year will visit feeding stations. The colder and snowier the weather, the larger the flocks of cardinals seem to be.

Of all the birds that visit backyard feeders, none is more familiar or more welcome than the cardinal. The crested crimson male is certainly one of the most widely recognized and admired birds in America. In fact, seven states have honored the cardinal by naming it the "state bird."

The male's brilliant red plumage and loud slurred whistles attract both attention and admiration from birdwatchers. But don't assume every singing cardinal is a male. Unlike most song birds, female cardinals sing, too.

Cardinals are easy to recognize because they are our only red-crested bird. The reddish brown female pales in comparison to the brilliant scarlet male. Adults of both sexes have bright pink or red bills and black faces. Juveniles resemble adults, but have dark bills.

Cardinal bills are massive and powerful. If ever a bird was meant to crack open and eat seeds, it's the cardinal. No wonder it is such a connoisseur of sunflower seeds.

Cardinals avoid deep forests and seem well adapted to habitat disturbances. Forest edges, old fields, parks, cemeteries and fencerows attract them throughout the year.

A better understanding of cardinal behavior comes from carefully observing what occurs at backyard bird feeders. Though the pair bond relaxes, mated cardinals remain together in small loose flocks during the winter. During intense cold snaps flocks of 10 to 20 birds sometime gather. Back in

January, during the "big freeze," I counted more than 50 in my backyard at one time.

Throughout the winter, males often eat their fill before allowing females access to the feeder. This behavior changes abruptly during spring courting, however. Then males not only permit females access to the feeder, they even husk the seeds and pass them, bill to bill, to the female. These "kisses" continue throughout the breeding season, serving to strengthen and maintain the bond.

One of the most interesting and commonly observed examples of cardinal behavior is their sometimes "crazed" attacks on windows. Usually in the spring (but I've had reports of this behavior in every season), seemingly suicidal cardinals repeatedly crash into large windows or glass patio doors. Occasionally casualties occur. Particularly aggressive cardinals can stun themselves or break their necks and die. If you find a stunned bird, put it in a paper bag, clip the bag securely and place it in a dark area for an hour. Then release the bird. Stunned birds usually recover quickly.

Why do cardinals abuse themselves so? Male cardinals are strongly territorial, even during the nonbreeding season. Although their aggressive tendencies subside during fall and winter, territorial outbursts can occur at any time.

When a male cardinal sees his reflection in a window or even a hubcap, he responds as if there is a real rival. Sometimes his attacks last for an hour or more until more powerful urges -- fatigue or hunger -- prevail.

Despite these occasional bouts of "insanity," cardinals retain their favorite bird status. At feeders, windows or just passing through the yard, cardinals invariably monopolize the spotlight.

My alarm goes off well before dawn each morning. It requires no batteries, winding or electricity. I wake each day to the chorus of birds outside the bedroom window.

On chilly nights I make sure the window is cracked so I won't miss the next morning's wake-up call. On warmer evenings I crank up the volume full blast by opening the window as far as it goes.

Often it's a house wren that first rouses me from sleep. His loud explosive song is an appropriate first call. He spits out a jumble of notes so fast they almost seem to stumble over each other. Then a turkey gobbles. A catbird mews. A downy woodpecker whinnies. And a red-eyed vireo preaches in its sing-song, conversational manner.

From the edge of the yard a Carolina wren belts out a series of triplets, "Tea kettle, tea kettle, tea kettle." At wood's edge a Kentucky warbler sings, "Chorry, chorry, chorry," accent on the second syllable. And from deeper in the woods, a wood thrush yodel, "Ee-o-lay," floats to the ridge top.

It's like roll call. I lay in bed until all my friends are present and accounted for. Only after I've recognized all the members of chorus do I feel obliged to rise.

One morning last May, I heard a song I couldn't identify. It was familiar. I just couldn't pull the name from that corner of my brain where "songs and their artists" are stored.

So I listened. Since it was new for the year, the singer was obviously a migrant. The song was complicated and musical; I couldn't put it into words. I listened more carefully, grateful for a reason to stay in bed just a bit longer. Then I noticed that each note was paired -- and the light bulb came on. Indigo bunting.

I should have recognized the song immediately if only because I go through this same routine each spring. I just need to remember that the song that I can never remember is the indigo bunting's. What makes this mental block even more frustrating is that indigo buntings are among the most common breeding birds on our ridge. Every old field hosts several pairs.

Upon recognizing the song, a flood of images flowed past my mind's eye.

Several key field marks help identify indigo buntings. About the size of a goldfinch and deep metallic blue in color, males are striking. Indigo blue is darker than bluebird blue. And as a favor to birdwatchers everywhere, male indigos sing from the tops of the highest trees, often from exposed dead branches. Scan the treetops in the direction of the song, and a spot of indigo quickly stands out.

The secretive females, on the other hand, stay hidden in the underbrush, where their drab brown color serves them well. The indigo nests I have found have been at eye level or below in blackberry or multiflora rose thickets. The female weaves a cup of dried grasses and bark strips and lines it with fine grasses, rootlets and, occasionally, animal fur.

She lays three or four unmarked white eggs and incubates them for about 12 days. The chicks remain in the nest for about 12 days after hatching. Mom tends to the business of raising the kids, while dad defends the territory from intruders and watches for predators. After the chicks fledge, the male helps feed the young. If the female starts a second nest, the male assumes complete responsibility for the first brood.

Suddenly, as if to break my concentration and urge me to get up, the male indigo flew close to the house and sang right outside the bedroom window. Mystery solved, my conscience translated the notes into words: "You've lazed long enough. Rise and shine!"

## Song Sparrows (2/91)

Warm, sunny March days signal the beginning of the end of winter. Dandelions and crocuses pop from the ground in what seems like the beat of a hummingbird wing. Swollen dogwood buds seem impatient for April when they can explode into bloom. And the birds that winter on my ridge can hardly contain themselves. I think they'd burst if they didn't sing on these bluebird winter days.

The most persistent late winter soloist in the fields that surround my house is the song sparrow. His loud, rich warbling song is difficult to describe, but once heard, easy to recognize. Sometimes it's easier to remember a bird song by attaching words to the notes, even if the translation is less than exact. When I hear, "Maids! Maids! Maids! Pick up the tea kettle, ettle, ettle," for example, I know a song sparrow is on patrol.

First from the top of a sumac, then from the corner of an old shed, and finally from atop a shaky old snag, he sings. His song tells neighboring males that this acre is his. And when females return in the spring, his song will stir potential mates. He may stay with one female all summer; or he may pair with a series of mates as the season progresses.

Song sparrows nest several times each year. They build their first on the ground amid the matted grass that cover the fields in early spring. Later, after trees and shrubs leaf out, females build their nests in bramble thickets or under the cover of a grape vine. Elevated nests are safer from the predators that roam below.

The simple nest itself is constructed of grasses, leaves, bark fibers and perhaps some hair. The female lays four or five eggs (though I once found a nest with seven eggs) and incubates them for 12 or 13 days. Mottled with brown markings, the eggs blend in well with the surrounding vegetation.

If the eggs survive the incubation period, the chicks face 10 more perilous days in the nest. Their chance of survival is low. Skunks, cats, raccoons, chipmunks, snakes, mice, crows, squirrels and blue jays see to that. Only 20 or 30 percent of all nests actually fledge young.

Song sparrows are on my mind because I often wake to their song at this time of year. And that reminds of me of the time I spent studying them in graduate school.

Most of what I know about song sparrows, however, is not from personal experience. It comes from the work of Margaret Morse Nice. This remarkable woman devoted much of her long life to ornithology, especially the study of song sparrows. Her research forms the basis for most of what we know about them. Even 19 years after her death at the age of 90, Nice is still known as "the song sparrow lady" and reigns as one of ornithology's shining stars.

Behaviorist Konrad Lorenz called her studies of the natural history of song sparrows, "a major break-through in the methods of studying animal behavior..... the first long term field investigation of the individual life of any free-living wild animal."

But the most amazing thing about Nice, and perhaps most inspiring to amateur naturalists everywhere, is that she had no formal training in ornithology. She was a wife, mother of four daughters and a child psychologist specializing in how children acquire language . She published 15 professional papers in the field.

Yet she is best remembered as one of the world's premier ornithologists. Harvard biologist Ernst Mayr wrote of her, "She almost single-handedly initiated a new era in American ornithology."

A housewife and child psychologist who studied song sparrows in the brushy old field next to her home near Columbus, Ohio, Nice is a wonderful role model for "amateur" naturalists who feel frustrated because they've had no formal training. Sometimes professionalism stems more from burning curiosity and dogged determination than a university degree.

## *Goldfinches* (8/93)

My dad called them wild canaries. The male's bright yellow body and long warbling song fit the name well. But when I bought my first field guide some 30 years ago, I discovered these common, familiar birds are more properly called American goldfinches.

Throughout the summer goldfinches spend most of their time in fencerows, old fields and wetlands. The bright yellow male, with its black crown, tail and wings, is easily recognized. The drabber olive female lacks the black crown.

Unlike most songbirds, which begin to nest in April or May, goldfinches delay nesting until July or even August. The nesting season often extends into September.

The timing of the nesting season is tied, at least in part, to the life cycles of wild thistle and milkweed. Goldfinches feast each year on the seeds of true native thistle seeds and use thistle and milkweed down to build nests.

A few weeks ago I noticed a drably colored female goldfinch fly along the edge of the yard. Not recognizing her at first, and thinking female warbler, I grabbed my binoculars for a closer look. The bird had landed in a sapling sassafras. Through the bright 8-power glass, I recognized her easily. What caught my eye was her bill stuffed with downy material. She was building a nest in the fork of the sapling about six feet above the ground.

The nest is easy to recognize. Goldfinches weave thistledown, milkweed down, and other plant fibers to form a deep cup. The nest is usually anchored to three or four stems of a small tree or shrub. The nest is woven so tightly that summer rains sometimes flood nests and drown chicks too small to keep above the water.

For the next three days I watched periodically as the female alone completed the nest. The male earned his keep defending their territory by singing and occasionally chasing away intruding males.

Then the pair disappeared. At first I thought they had abandoned the nest. When they returned three days later, the female laid the first of five white eggs. Perhaps goldfinches leave a newly built nest to divert the attention of predators away from an obvious hub of activity.

For the next 12 days the female incubated her clutch faithfully. Her mate visited regularly and fed her mouthfuls of partly digested seeds. Unlike many birds, which switch to insect foods during the breeding season, goldfinches stick almost exclusively to a diet of seeds. They even feed their nestlings regurgitated seeds.

On day 12, the eggs hatched. For the first few days, mom brooded the helpless, naked chicks and dad provided meals. After the chicks were big enough to generate some body heat, the female began feeding them, too.

By the time the chicks were 10 days old, they looked like goldfinches. Thanks to their parents' attentiveness, the nest literally bulged with goldfinches. When the fledglings left the nest, the male continued to feed them until they could feed themselves.

As the nesting season winds down and fall colors begin to appear, goldfinches molt. That is, they replace their worn, tattered feathers with a fresh, new set.

The appearance of males changes drastically during molt. The brilliant yellow body feathers are replaced by dull brownish plumes, and the striking black cap disappears. Females also molt, but their appearance doesn't change. These are the drab little goldfinches that visit winter feeders.

The fall molt adds hundreds of feathers to the goldfinch's winter plumage. This extra insulation helps keep them warm on cold winter days and nights. In the spring goldfinches molt again, and males regain their breeding colors. And so it goes.

## Sunflowers                                          (1/92)

- Prehistoric Native Americans were the first humans to eat sunflowers seeds.
- Russian immigrants in Canada "reintroduced" sunflower seeds as a human food to North America.
- Sunflowers seeds, the single most popular wild bird food, are a by-product of the confection seed and oil-seed markets.

These are just a few of the kernels of sunflower trivia I've picked up over the years as I've studied the wild bird food business. Though people who feed birds tend to be preoccupied with the visitors at backyard bird feeders, the story behind the foods is a fascinating one as well.

Archaeologists report that sunflowers seeds were first used and cultivated by prehistoric Indian tribes in what is now the U.S. southwest. They were eaten and used in religious rituals and as decorations on utensils and baskets.

In the 16th century Spanish explorers took sunflowers seeds back to Europe. They slowly spread across the continent and were used primarily for ornamental purposes for several hundred years. It took the Russians to recognize their food value.

The Russian Orthodox church forbade the eating of oil-rich foods during the 40 days preceding both Christmas and Easter.

Because sunflowers were new and unfamiliar, they were not on the list of forbidden foods. The working class welcomed this new source of meal and oil. By the mid-1850s many Russian farmers raised sunflowers, and even today Russia remains the world's leading producer of sunflower seeds.

In the 1870s Russian immigrants who had settled on the plains of what is now Manitoba and Saskatchewan raised Russian Mammoth sunflowers on their farms. By the 1880s U.S. seed companies were selling Russian Mammoths in their catalogs.

Fifty years later U.S. sunflower production averaged about six million pounds annually. In 1991, for example, U.S. farmers planted nearly 2.5 million acres of sunflowers for a total production of 1.5 million metric tons of sunflower seeds (average yield: 1,338 pounds per acre). North Dakota (1.6 million acres) led the U.S. in sunflower production, followed by South Dakota (427,000 acres) and Minnesota (280,000 acres).

Though the percentages vary from year to year, 75 to 85 percent of total production is black- oil seed. The balance is striped or confection seeds. Ironically, both types of sunflowers are raised primarily for human consumption. Oil seeds are pressed to produce sunflower oil; confection seeds are marketed primarily as snack foods -- roasted both in and out of the shells. Most confection type seeds are exported to Europe (primarily Spain and Germany), but they're gaining popularity in the U.S. among professional athletes as a tobacco substitute.

The bird seed market is secondary and generally gets the seeds that are graded unfit for human consumption. The primary standard for quality is size. Seeds for the bird food market are nutritionally as good as those for human use, they're just smaller. By allocating low grade seeds to the bird food market, seed traders improve their profit margins or at least minimize their losses.

Finally, on a more practical note, if you have ever examined sunflower seeds carefully, you've probably noticed that many of the seeds have tiny holes in them. Holes clearly made by insects. Fear not. Those holes were not made by an insect entering the seed to destroy it. They were made by insect larvae leaving the seed. They are exit holes.

Seed weevils, which are small beetles, lay their eggs (one per seed) in the developing seed before the shell forms. After hatching, the grub eats a portion of the seed, then burrows through the seed hull and drops to the ground where it overwinters in the soil. The important point is that seed weevils rarely consume the entire seed. The portion that remains is fine for birds.

That's the story behind the seed.


## Melons (7/95)

"Who died and made you the watermelon expert?"

Linda was obviously annoyed. This was her domain. During our 20 years of marriage, she has fussed about watermelons every summer. She loves watermelons. That's the problem. She loves all watermelons -- long ones, round ones, light ones, dark ones. If it's a watermelon, it's got to be good.

I'm more discriminating. So when she raved about the melon she just cut and tasted, I sampled a piece. It was delicious -- ruby red flesh and sweet as sugar. But the texture wasn't quite right. It wasn't sandy, but neither was it as crisp as it could be. That was my only comment. It seemed innocent enough to me, but apparently Linda took offense.

I cut a seed-free filet from the center of my piece and placed it on her plate. In our house nothing soothes a riled spouse quicker than a chunk of seedless watermelon.

The incident got me thinking about melons and their natural history. Neither watermelons nor cantaloupes are native to North America. Explorers introduced them to the continent in the 16th century. Watermelons were introduced from Africa; cantaloupes came from Persia. Most varieties, of which there are dozens, do best in a hot, dry climate, though some cultivars do well in temperate areas. Depending on the variety, most melons require 65 to 90 days to mature.

In my search for melon facts, I was also surprised to learn that melons are members of the cucumber family. I shouldn't have been. Both their growth form, a vine, and their flowers are quite similar to cucumbers.

The clean-up that follows a melon-fest is quick and easy. We cut up the rinds and toss them on the compost pile. They decay quickly and help activate overall decomposition.

And then there are the seeds. So many seeds. Air dry them on a sheet of butcher paper, then store them in a cool, dry place. Do this with pumpkins and squash, too. Many seed-eating birds love melon seeds. That's why some better bird food mixes now include melon and/or squash seeds. Look for them on the ingredients list.

Cardinals, grosbeaks, blue jays, chickadees, nuthatches, towhees and doves are just some of the feeder birds that eat melon seeds. Run the dried seeds once through a meat grinder to make the kernels easier for some of the smaller birds to extract.

People, of course, prefer the flesh.

What makes a perfect watermelon? In my mind, it's simple. It must be ripe, sweet, and crisp. The first cut through the rind should crack. I also like my watermelon cold -- ice cold. A refrigerator will do, but five or six hours in a tub of ice is even better.

Unfortunately, perfect melons are hard to come by. In season, we buy several each week. I judge a watermelon by holding it up to one ear and thumping it. If the stem is dry and it sounds like it's full of water, I buy it. Most are good, many are very good, but I count myself lucky if I taste more than one five-star melon each summer. Picking superior watermelons is an art that requires decades of practice and testing. So I keep buying and tasting.

I can also make a case for cantaloupes. They rank second only to watermelons as my favorite fruit, but excellent 'loupes seem easier to find. A good, ripe cantaloupe smells like a good, ripe cantaloupe. A spoon slips through ripe cantaloupe flesh like a warm knife through butter. The best I've tasted come from eastern Ohio Amish country. There they grow bigger than any other cantaloupes I've ever seen, and the flesh is always orange and sweet. And in one of those maddening inconsistencies that drives my wife crazy, I prefer eating cantaloupes at room temperature.

Melons are one of nature's perfect foods -- sweet, filling and delicious. Even the rinds and seeds need not be wasted.

Two years ago my wife and I encountered a strange organism while canoeing in Pennsylvania. We noticed peculiar gelatinous masses attached in shallow water to stumps and logs. Some were as large as footballs. Viewed from above the surface of the water, they appeared fuzzy.

At first I thought these were fish or amphibian egg masses. I tried to grab one. It was indeed gelatinous and very slippery. Finally, using the blades of our paddles, Linda and I managed to hoist it into the canoe.

I examined it carefully and quickly ruled out any sort of vertebrate egg mass. I could see no developing embryos; it had to be an invertebrate. The outer surface was covered with what appeared to be irregularly shaped, textured plates. They were slightly rough to the touch.

I then sliced it open with a pocket knife. The inside was pure jelly. Whatever this creature was, its living parts were restricted to the textured plates on the "blob's" exterior. We made notes describing its appearance so we would be able to describe it to someone who knew more about this than we did.

When we returned home, I consulted my invertebrate zoology textbooks. Eventually I concluded that the blob was a bryozoan. Unfortunately this wasn't terribly helpful, because bryozoans are a rather obscure group of invertebrates. They merited just a few short pages in a very large textbook.

By this time I had become mildly obsessed with identifying the blob. I paged through every book in my library that I thought might shed some light. Finally I came to a seldom used field guide to freshwater life, and there it was -- a photograph of my creature. It was indeed a bryozoan; one named *Pectinatella magnifica*. Sadly, though, the book provided little information about *Pectinatella* natural history.

An invertebrate biology textbook published in 1991 finally led me to an expert. Dr. Tim Wood, a biologist at Wright State University in Dayton, Ohio, wrote the chapter on bryozoans. When I finally tracked him down and called him at his lab, I told him my tale and asked if he could enlighten me. Turns out Dr. Wood is one of the few bryozoan experts in the country, and *Pectinatella* is one of his favorite organisms.

The "blobs, " he told me, were actually colonies of thousands of individuals called zoids. Each of the textured plates I had originally noticed consisted of several zoids.

"Under a microscope," Wood explained, "each zoid looks like a flower -- the 'petals' being tiny tentacles that capture food particles suspended in the water. The zoids eat plankton and organic debris. It was the tentacles that gave your 'blob' its fuzzy underwater appearance."

The "blob" itself was a gelatinous mass produced by the zoids simply so they would have something to attach themselves to. The jelly is more than 99 percent water and contains a protein similar to egg albumen.

By the end of the summer the zoids produce statoblasts, tiny burr-like offspring analogous to plant seeds. The statoblasts stick to the fur of mammals and feathers of birds and get carried to different parts of the lake, different lakes, or even different states.

The *Pectinatella* colony cannot survive cold temperatures, so it overwinters in the statoblast stage. The statoblasts remain dormant until spring. Then they "germinate" into individual zoids. The zoids grow and reproduce rapidly until by mid-summer new gelatinous colonies can be found attached to stumps in lakes.

*Pectinatella's* ecological value is unclear. By eating organic debris it may purify or at least clarify turbid water. Dr. Wood also told me that the larvae of several species of midges live in *Pectinatella* colonies, but he knows of nothing that eats *Pectinatella*. It is harmless to people -- the tentacles do not sting. But some individuals may be allergic to the slime that covers the outer surface.

Though poorly understood, *Pectinatella's* natural history illustrates the fascinating complexities of even the most primitive forms of life.

If you sleep with the windows open, you know that you needn't leave home to hear the music of the night. Nature echoes with the sounds of nocturnal phantoms.

In early spring frogs herald the end of winter. In May and June, owls, whip-poor-wills and over zealous mockingbirds join the night time list of songsters. Summer's end, however, brings the most incessant chorus of the year. It is now that orthopterans monopolize the nightly serenade.

Orthopterans include the group of insects we commonly refer to as crickets and grasshoppers. Everyone knows the familiar black field cricket that lives in backyards everywhere. And I'm sure that I'm not the only one who has spent half an evening on a search and destroy mission for the rogue cricket that found its way into the house and what it perceived as the perfect music hall. From a distance the field cricket's high pitched trill is soothing and pastoral. But in the bedroom even a solitary cricket song breeds insanity.

Another widely recognized sound of late summer is the song of the katydid. Katydids are large green grasshoppers. They often come to night lights on the back porch. Their green textured outer wings look like leaves and provide almost perfect camouflage for hiding in the bushes by day. Katydids also have extremely long antennae that arch backward over the length of the body.

But the best way to recognize a katydid is by ear at night. Males sing from early evening well into the night. The song is harsh and burry and sounds something like "Ch-ch" or "Ch-ch-ch" or "ch-ch-ch-ch." The phrases are repeated about once a second, and the rhythm suggests the insect's name: Ka-ty, ka-ty-did or kay-ty-did-did. Occasionally several individuals sing in unison to form a genuine chorus. In fact, as I prepared for writing this column one night, I reviewed some recorded insect sounds, and two or three real katydids outside the window sang in sync with the tape after just a few phrases.

The singer of the most familiar summer nocturnes remains a mystery to most people. Snowy tree crickets generate a seemingly endless series of high-pitched melodic chirps that to many almost define a summer night. This is the insect that is sometimes called the "thermometer cricket" -- count the number of chirps in 15 seconds, add 40 and you have the temperature in Fahrenheit. I've tested this old saw, however, and suffice it to say, I'll stick with a thermometer.

Though often heard and recognized, snowy tree crickets are almost impossible to find without a diligent search. During the day they feed and rest amidst the foliage of trees and shrubs. Thanks to their small size and cryptic pale green color, they blend in with their surroundings. And at night, their song has a ventriloquistic effect. Shine a light where you think the tree cricket must be and sure enough it's not. It takes good eyes, patient scanning and a little luck to find a tree cricket.

The common link among these orthopteran songsters is how they produce the sounds we hear. The process is call stridulation -- rubbing one body part against another. In the cases of the orthopterans I've described, the body parts in question are the front wings. To "sing," they elevate their front wings and move them back and forth. Where the wings overlap, a sharp edge (the scraper) on one wing rubs against a file-like ridge (the file) on the other. Membranes on the wing act as a sounding board to amplify the sound. The process is not unlike the sound that resonates from the body of a violin when the bow is pulled across the strings.

Despite what you may read elsewhere, you need not travel to New York or Toronto to hear the music of the night. Just keep your windows open, and it will come to you.

## *Monarch Butterflies* (8/94)

CAPE MAY, New Jersey -- As I walked along the beach recently, migration was on my mind. It was early, August 10th to be exact, but already shorebirds had begun passing through. Sanderlings played tag with the waves, ruddy turnstones rested on the beach and least sandpipers flew up and down the shore in groups of six to 10 birds. In groups of twos and threes great egrets passed overhead, perhaps on their way to Delaware. And a lone brown pelican sailed south along the coast.

On the sand dunes just a hundred yards from the ocean, another more subtle migration was underway. A steady stream of monarch butterflies fluttered by. Some stopped periodically to sip nectar from the many colorful wildflowers that dot the dunes. Their passage reminded me that birds are not the only animals that migrate. Monarchs are equally renowned for their annual long distance movements.

Each summer and fall these colorful orange and black insects migrate south for the winter. Western populations winter along the southern California coast, while monarchs east of the Rockies migrate to the Gulf Coast or central Mexico. Mark and recapture studies have shown that monarchs travel as far as 1,800 miles in just four months. They move only by day at a leisurely pace of five to 18 mph.

Not only do monarchs travel great distances, they do so with unerring accuracy. Year after year they return to the same winter areas, even the same trees. So reliable are these migratory aggregations that they have become major tourist attractions in Mexico and southern California. The town of Pacific Grove, Calif., for example, proudly calls itself "Butterfly City, U.S.A."

What makes the monarch migration even more amazing is that each butterfly makes the trip only once. Monarchs that return in the spring lay eggs, then die. Consequently, one to several generations of monarchs separate those that return in the spring from those that depart in the fall. Yet somehow each fall, inexperienced monarchs return to their ancestors' traditional wintering areas. Some researchers suggest that genetic olfactory cues could provide the guidance system.

On the winter grounds monarchs are sluggish and inactive. They congregate on tree trunks by the millions. During the winter the monarchs use very little of their fat reserves. When February rolls around, they still have plenty of stored energy for the trip north. Mating occurs before migration begins, and females lay eggs as they move northward. This insures a new generation of monarchs as far as the females survive.

Monarchs occur throughout temperate North America. Their life cycle is a textbook example of complete insect metamorphosis. Females lay clusters of pinhead-sized eggs on the undersides of leaves of milkweed plants. In three to 12 days the eggs hatch.

Tiny, ravenous caterpillars emerge. Bold black, white, and yellow rings encircle the body and identify the fleshy larval stage. Within 14 days they devour enough milkweed leaves to weigh more than 2,000 times their hatching weight.

Each caterpillar then finds a protected perch and molts into a cocoon-like pupal case called a chrysalis. Over the next two to three weeks, the contents of the pale-green, gold-flecked chrysalis transforms from a lowly caterpillar into the beautiful burnt-orange adult butterfly.

Beautiful as they may be, however, most monarch larva and adults taste terrible to anything that eats them. In laboratory experiments blue jays vomit within minutes of eating a monarch.

Why? Because monarchs are what they eat. Many species of milkweed are highly toxic. Though monarchs are unaffected by the toxin, they incorporate the poison into their own body tissues. The poison is retained through metamorphosis so even adults have high concentrations of the toxins.

Curiously, the toxin is more highly concentrated in the wings than in the body. Thus, a predator that nips even a piece of wing discovers that monarchs are distasteful. This enables predators to learn that monarchs taste badly without necessarily killing the butterfly. This also explains why we often see monarchs with badly battered wings -- battle scars from the ongoing struggle between predator and prey.

## Tent Caterpillars (6/95)

There is no more ordinary creature than the eastern tent caterpillar. At this time of year their distinctive silky tents can be found in woods, old fields and along country roads. Yet their life history is as extraordinary and mysterious as any of their lepidopteran kin.

It's hard to know where to begin the story. Tent caterpillars spend most of their lives inside an egg. Adult moths live just a few days. The form we know best, the caterpillar, is the most conspicuous.

Let's fast forward to late June or early July. A small brown moth struggles free from a cocoon fastened to the inside of a slab of loose bark on an old dying tree. Blood courses through its unfurling wings; within a few hours the one-and-a-half inch moth is on the wing. It wanders purposely, led by olfactory cues, in search of a mate. Within 48 hours, the female is bred. Now she searches for apple, cherry and other fruit trees. She deposits a cluster of 200 to 300 eggs around a small twig. Their responsibilities satisfied, adult males and females die just a few days after emerging from the cocoon.

The moth's destiny now lies inside the egg case that hardens on the twig. Through the blistering heat of summer and the frigid cold of winter, the eggs lay dormant, shielded from the elements only by the egg case's thin protective membrane. Thanks to a natural antifreeze called glycerol, which makes up 35 percent of the egg's weight by January, the fluids in the embryo remain unfrozen.

Inside the egg, a biological clock ticks, marking off the months until spring's longer days trigger the clock's alarm. The eggs hatch in April and tiny, hungry caterpillars emerge. They migrate downward toward a centrally located crotch in the tree and begin spinning and weaving the familiar tent. The caterpillars work in shifts to build a shelter that consists of many horizontal layers, not unlike a dish of lasagna or baklava. The space between each layer is just large enough to accommodate a group of caterpillars.

When not resting or building the tent, tent caterpillars march upward along the tree's smallest branches in search of fresh tender leaves. Their eat voraciously and grow rapidly. To insure that they can find their way back to the tent, tent caterpillars leave behind a trail of silk. The combined efforts of the colony yield an extensive network of silky trails that always lead home. If Hansel and Gretel had been so skilled, the Brothers Grimm would have had one less fairy tale to tell.

Insect growth is limited by an elastic exoskeleton that can stretch only so far. It then splits, and the old exoskeleton is shed. Tent caterpillars molt six times from April through June. Each time hormones control the process to insure that a new, larger caterpillar, rather than a premature moth, results.

After the final molt, the concentration of juvenile hormone ebbs so that when the mature caterpillar attains a certain critical weight, the next transformation is far more dramatic. At this critical size, other hormones kick in. Caterpillars lose their appetite and wander in search of a place to pupate. This is when we see them crossing roads, trails and lawns.

Under a log, a rock or a slab of bark, the tent caterpillar undergoes its final and most miraculous transformation. First, it weaves itself a silky cocoon, being careful to leave a weak spot from which its final incarnation can emerge. Over the course of the next three weeks, the caterpillar physiologically and biochemically transforms itself from hairy caterpillar to scale-covered moth.

Adult moths have a single purpose -- reproduction. That done, the short-lived moths die, and a new generation of eggs awaits the following spring. It's an extraordinary story for such an ordinary creature.

## *Brook Trout* (5/93)

This "fish story" began in the fall. Shorter days and colder water temperatures triggered hormonal changes in the brook trout that inhabit clear, cold waterways. Males' bellies and lower fins turned crimson. The blue-haloed red spots that dot the brookies' sides sparkled. Bright white bands lined the edges of the fins. And their lower jaws grew and turned upward, though not as obviously as other members of the salmon family.

The outward appearance of the females changed little. Inside, however, females turned into egg-making machines.

Brook trout spawn in the fall. When the forests blaze in autumnal glory, signaling the onset of winter dormancy for many creatures, brook trout renew the annual creative ritual that perpetuates the species.

Along the shores of beaver ponds, small rivers and even the tiniest spring-fed mountain streams, females choose the spawning site. The gravel and stones that will hold the eggs must be rather large -- one to 10 inches in diameter. The water must be between 40 and 55 degrees F. And most importantly, there must be an upwelling of ground water directly beneath the nest or at least a current to carry away silt and sediments.

When a female finds a site that meets her requirements, she builds the nest, or "redd," as ichthyologists call it. She nestles herself tightly against the stream bed and anchors herself with her caudal fin. Then she violently swims in place, writhing her body back and forth. The hydraulics of her movements create a saucer in the gravel and stir up a cloud of debris -- tiny particles of sediment, organic matter and insects that get swept away by the current. A clean nest enables oxygenated water to bathe the eggs after spawning.

The female's nest-building activity attracts males to the redd. While the female toils, the males establish a dominance hierarchy based on size, aggressive displays and bouts that may include butting, nipping and biting. The largest male usually wins breeding rights.

When the female is ready to spawn, she drags her anal fin through the redd. This attracts the dominant male's attention, and he swims by her side. In an act that lasts barely three or four seconds, the female opens her mouth widely and arches her back. Likewise, the male gapes, and a shiver-like action wracks his body. Simultaneously, the female releases her eggs, and the male discharges a dose of milt (sperm). The milky cloud settles into the redd. The spawn is complete.

The male leaves immediately, perhaps to search for another mate. The female completes the redd by using her fins to shovel a load of clean gravel atop the fertilized eggs. The eggs are now hidden, safe and ready for a winter of dormancy. The sediment-free redd keep the eggs well oxygenated during the winter months. A few days later the female builds a new redd and repeats the ritual.

The eggs hatch in early March. The fry work their way up through the gravel and establish small feeding territories amid the rocks and debris that litter the stream bottom. Small fry eat plankton; fingerlings switch to larger prey such as aquatic insects and other invertebrates.

The rate of growth of young brook trout varies with habitat. In lakes and beaver ponds brook trout can reach three to four pounds in three years. But in cold mountain streams, a seven-inch brookie is considered a trophy. And that's what fly fishing purists hope for when they wet a line in a mountain stream small enough to cross in one step.

It's OK to look askance at the hatchery-reared rainbow and brown trout most anglers pull from the publicly stocked waterways. Instead, honor the brook trout -- the east's only native trout.




## Gray Tree Frogs (7/96)

Another cool, rainy evening during an uncommonly cool, rainy summer greets nightfall. I step onto the porch for a listen. I hear only raindrops. No crickets, no owls; just raindrops.

Then a familiar sound cuts through the darkness. I immediately think screech-owl because the sound is a monotone trill. But it's too short for a screech-owl. This trill lasts only a second or so. Then I hear it again. And again. Soon I'm hearing the short trill every few seconds.

It's a new sound for the ridge. Probably because I've just never noticed it before, not because the singer is new. My brain goes into search mode to retrieve the sound stored somewhere on my mind's hard drive. I know I've heard the sound before, but retrieval is slow. Finally, the name materializes. Gray tree frog. Slowly my memory provides more details. Over the years I've heard it in Georgia, Oklahoma, Maine and Pennsylvania.

The first time was in Georgia's Okefenokee Swamp. It was during an extended college field trip to catch, see and hear critters. They sang us to sleep as mosquitoes buzzed inside the tents. In Oklahoma it was again on a field trip to the northeastern part of the state that I heard this frog, only this time I was an instructor rather than a student. In Maine the sound came from a single tree in a huge paved parking lot. I actually caught this one, but never figured out how or why it made its way to this inhospitable island. In Pennsylvania, I've heard gray tree frogs in many state parks.

What's notable about these recollections is that I've heard many gray tree frogs, but seen few. And that's typical. Gray tree frogs, when silent, are nearly invisible. By day, they hide inside dark cool tree cavities or behind slabs of bark. At night they emerge to eat, sing and mate. When gray tree frogs are abundant, their chorus can be quite noisy.

Sticky adhesive pads on their toes enable them to cling tightly to tree trunks and branches. There they wait patiently and silently for tasty flies, beetles, caterpillars, aphids and moths.

Though most breeding occurs by early June, gray tree frogs sing throughout the summer, especially on cool, wet nights. If ever you find one, you'll be impressed by the big sound that comes from such a small creature. Gray tree frogs usually measure less than two inches in length, and their appearance varies. Depending on light, temperature, moisture, temperature, stress or activity level, they may be gray, green or brown. Thanks to this cryptic coloration, they are extremely difficult to spot, even during the day. Two fairly reliable field marks, however, are bright orange inner hind legs and, unlike most frogs, course skin. Their body is quite warty, though the individual warts are much smaller than those found on toads.

Gray tree frogs leave the safety of trees for the ground for only two reasons.

Like most amphibians, they gather at water's edge to make more tree frogs. Responding to the males' song, females find males to invite a mating embrace called amplexus. As a female releases as many as 1,000 individual eggs, the male fertilizes them. The eggs drift downward or float away and eventually settle on aquatic vegetation, sticks or other submerged debris. In six to 12 days, depending on water temperature, the eggs hatch into tadpoles with red tails. In two to three months, again depending on temperature, the tadpoles transform into small frogs.

As winter approaches, gray tree frogs leave their arboreal refuge to seek shelter under logs or leaf litter. There they remain dormant until spring, when their cycle of life resumes.

As the bulldozer leveled a small piece of ground just above the house, I expected at least one creature would be dislodged from a burrow. The only question was which one. Shortly after the dozer operator turned off the machine to take a break, I had my answer. It was a snake.

It was dark rusty brown, mottled and about 30 inches long. The operator warned me to stay clear. It was a copperhead, he said. I stepped closer. No, it's a milk snake, I countered.

Back and forth we bantered until finally I had no choice. I stepped even closer and made sure the head was not triangular and the pupils not vertical. Then I picked it up. For a few moments it struggled, but it quickly calmed down. The neck was not constricted behind the head to form a triangular head. In hand, the pupils were clearly round. And there were no pits between the yes and nostrils. Definitely not a copperhead. They, like other pit vipers (which includes rattlesnakes) have triangular heads, vertical pupils and prominent heat sensing pits between the eyes and nostrils. This was a beneficial, nonvenomous milk snake.

At a glance, milk snakes and copperheads superficially resemble each other. The basic color of each is rusty brown, but the copperhead has a much richer copper tone. The milk snake is a drabber brown. Furthermore, both species have dark bands that cross over the back and reach down the sides. The milk snake's "saddles" are bordered in black and are widest across the back. Often they become narrower as they reach down the sides. The copperhead's saddles, on the other hand, are most narrow on the back and wider on the sides. They have an hourglass shape.

A third unmistakable difference between milk snakes and copperheads can be found on their bellies. The copperhead's is unmarked and cream colored. A milk snake's white belly is marked with black squares that creates a checkerboard effect.

I admit these characteristics cannot be seen from too far away. But if you're close enough to chop a snake with a hoe or shovel, you're close enough to detect head shape. I understand people's desire to rid their backyards of poisonous copperheads, but I suspect that many of the "copperheads" killed each year are milk snakes or even juvenile black rat snakes, which sometimes display a mottled pattern on their backs.

Just a few weeks ago, for example, a local television station aired a report of a huge "copperhead" found nearby. The footage clearly showed a five-foot long adult black rat snake. Those few seconds of videotape reinforced the misinformation that abounds about copperheads.

Though the subject of snakes is distasteful to many, here are a few points to ponder.

• Most snakes, even poisonous ones, are beneficial. They eat mostly insects, mice, rats and other small rodents.

• Snakes are shy and retiring. Their instinct is to slither away when disturbed, not attack. The best way to get bitten is to disturb a snake that has no escape route. To avoid accidental encounters with snakes, watch where you place your hands and feet when roaming the woods and fields. Be especially careful in rocky areas.

• Though copperheads are more common and widespread than rattlesnakes, their bite is much less dangerous. That's because copperheads are smaller, they deliver less venom and their venom is weaker than rattlesnake venom. I know of no human deaths caused by copperhead bites.

• Treat any poisonous snake bite seriously. Keep the victim calm and quiet, and get him to the nearest hospital as soon as possible.

• If you spend anytime outdoors this summer, you will probably encounter a snake. It will probably be a harmless garter, ribbon, ringneck, green, rat or milk snake. If you don't provoke the snake, it will not strike. Simply walk around it.

# Opossums

"Time to play 'possum, Daddy!"

My girls and I have been "playing 'possum" a lot since last spring. That's when we adopted five orphaned baby opossums. Almost every day we played with the babies, who are now almost full grown.

I have wanted a possum for several years now -- ever since a reader from the Harrisburg area wrote and told me she had raised a 'possum from infancy. She said it was the best pet she ever had -- clean, house-broken, gentle, affectionate. It cuddled on her lap at night while she watched television.

Back in May opportunity knocked. A neighbor phoned and said she rescued a litter of baby 'possums from her dog. Several hours had passed and the mother was no where to be found, so we presumed her dead. The babies needed attention warmth and food, so I picked them up.

I could cradle all five in one hand. They weighed in about two ounces each, making them approximately 70 days old. Based on their weight, they had been born back in early March. They were furred and their eyes open, but they were scarcely big enough to be out of the mother's pouch.

They looked like small rats -- black beady eyes, pointy snout, huge naked ears and a long scaly tail. After feeding them a few meals of strained beef baby food ("injected" with a needle-less syringe), I noticed how tidy they were. After each meal they washed they face and hands just like mice do. They soiled their bedding a night, but they were, after all, still very young.

As time passed I varied their diet -- they loved strained meat, fruit and vegetable baby food, pork chop bones, grapes and cat food. Then, after dinner, they'd all cram into my shirt pockets and snooze while I watched the evening news.

The third graders at the local elementary school loved them when I visited my daughter's class. And even they appreciated the miracle of marsupial reproduction. After just a 13-day pregnancy, as many as 25 naked, blind, bumble bee-sized young climb to their mother's pouch, using well-developed forelimbs and claws to move through her fur. The journey takes just 20 seconds.

In the pouch it's first-come, first-served. Females have only 13 nipples, so at most only 13 young survive. Usually, however, only five to eight make it to the pouch. There they remain for about eight weeks until weaned. Then they spend several weeks riding on mom's back while she teaches them the meaning of 'possum life. That's about the time I entered this story.

Summer raced by, and while my family and I traveled to North Dakota, one of my daughter's friends took care of the "kids." She did a great job -- they nearly doubled in size during the three weeks we were away.

They are now nearly fully grown -- at least big enough to defend themselves from marauding cats. They are still affectionate and admirably clean. They keep their fur luxuriously soft and their fleshy hands and feet are always well scrubbed. And as adults, they never soil their sleeping quarters.

One now lives in luxury at the local zoo. The others I'll soon release and hope they'll adopt a nest box on the back porch as home base. But no doubt they'll disperse. Adult opossums lead solitary lives.

I've come to truly appreciate that letter from the Harrisburg woman. It's not that I "love" these animals in a sentimental way. But I have developed a deep affection for them. And they seem to like me, too.

Now when I see road-killed 'possums, I no longer snicker and make dumb 'possum jokes. Instead I think fondly of five of the neatest little creatures I've ever known.

When my family and I returned from a few weeks of travel last summer, I intended to carry our bags into the house before darkness fell, but I got sidetracked with mail and phone messages. In the confusion I left the front door ajar.

A few hours later, after darkness had fallen, I sat in the living room reading the newspaper. Out of the corner of my eye, I saw something flutter. I assumed it was a large moth. It wasn't.

It soon appeared again, this time swooping just in front of the newspaper. It was a small bat. It must have entered the house while I had the door propped open. I called to my daughters, and they came into the room. After the initial shock and few shrieks, they stood with me and watched the bat wheel expertly back and forth across the room. Then I turned out the lights. I wanted to show Nora and Emma that the bat would not attack us or even get very close to us. It didn't. Using its radar-like echolocation system, it skillfully avoided all obstacles, including us.

Practicing what I preach, I opened the front door to give the bat a chance to find its own escape route. After a few minutes, the bat disappeared. I assumed it had found its way outside. I was wrong. A familiar, blood-curdling scream from upstairs told me so.

Linda was just about to step into the shower when the bat ascended the staircase and found its way to the bathroom. Under the circumstances, Linda was in no mood for a natural history lesson, so I chased the bat into Emma's room and opened the windows. Surely, it would "echolocate" its way out.

Ten minutes later I poked my head into the room. The bat now hung upside down from the wooden wall next to Emma's bed. It was still, probably tired and did not move when I approached, so I told the girls it was time to try plan B.

I retrieved a butterfly net from my office. Then I walked up the bat and quickly placed the mouth of the net over the it. When the bat dropped off the wall to escape, it fell immediately into the net. (If a butterfly net had not been handy, I could have just as easily placed a wide-mouthed canning jar over the bat, then slid a piece of cardboard between the jar and wall.)

Before releasing the bat, I had the girls take a closer look. In flight, it seemed large and sinister; its wingspan was about 10 inches. In the net, however, this little brown bat (*Myotis lucifugus*), the most common and widespread species in North America, was barely three inches long. When Nora described it as "just a mouse with wings," she couldn't have come up with more appropriate description.

Through the fine material of the net, I extended the wings to show the girls that elongated finger bones give bat wings their size and shape. I also pointed out the disproportionately large ears responsible for their acute hearing.

Then we stepped outside, and I unfurled the net. The bat flew into the night, the girls had another wildlife tale and I had something to write about.

Every year bats appear in thousands of homes on warm summer nights, and every year many of those home owners respond hysterically. Slowly, as word of the value of bats gets out, people are becoming more educated and tolerant.

Consider, for example, the city of Austin, Texas. When the Congress Avenue Bridge was rebuilt back in 1980, it became a source of fear and loathing. The rebuilt bridge contained many small expansion joints that averaged three-quarters inch across -- the ideal crevice width for roosting Mexican free-tailed bats. The bats, which previously roosted under the bridge in small numbers, decided the new Congress Avenue Bridge made an ideal maternity roost. Soon hundreds of thousands of bats roosted under the bridge. Each evening around dusk, the bats left the bridge to feed. Their nightly emergence drew lots of attention, much of it negative. Fear and ignorance of the value of bats led people to demand that the bat colony be eradicated.

That's when Dr. Merlin Tuttle, founder and executive director of Bat Conservation International (BCI), stepped in. He explained to anyone who would listen that bats are gentle, biologically sophisticated animals that should be welcome in any community. On a typical summer evening these bridge bats would eat 10,000 to 30,000 pounds of flying insects. Over the course of a south Texas summer, that adds up to hundreds of tons of insects. Imagine the economic savings and public health benefits associated with a large bat colony in terms of reduction of pesticide use. Furthermore, the citizens of Austin learned that if they never handled a bat, they had virtually no chance of contracting any diseases. (Yes, bats can carry rabies, but no more commonly than any other mammal.)

Over time, Austin accepted the bats at the Congress Avenue Bridge. Today the colony has grown to 1.5 million bats. The nightly emergence has become a major tourist attraction. Hundreds and often thousands of people come to the bridge every night to watch the bats emerge. Window tables at nearby restaurants fill quickly. This is a perfect example of how education, cooperation and understanding can turn a perceived liability into a tremendous asset.

Over the last few years, BCI biologists have identified 59 other Texas bridges that shelter bat roosts during the breeding season. They now get inquiries from other states asking how to attract bats to bridges.

Another man-made habitat that bats use is abandoned mines. Old mine shafts are a safety hazard and a liability to mining companies, so increasingly they are capped, filled or collapsed. This not only ruins mines as bat habitat, it can also entomb and kill thousands or even millions of bats.

In 1992, for example, a million bats were discovered hibernating in a mine scheduled to be closed in northern Michigan. It was the second largest colony of hibernating bats ever found in North America. BCI stepped in and explained the value of bats to the local community and mining officials. Instead of closing the mine, which can be a costly procedure, BCI convinced officials to put a metal "gate" on the mine opening. The gate allows bats to enter and leave freely, but keeps people out. Tuttle calls it a "win, win, win situation." The mining company saves money and knows people cannot enter the mine, the local community learns that conservation and industry are not necessarily incompatible and the bats are left undisturbed.

Similar results have been achieved elsewhere. In Pennsylvania a closed mine in Canoe Creek State Park was reopened in time to save the state's largest population of hibernating bats. In Wisconsin two gated mines saved more than 600,000 bats. In New Jersey the state's largest population of hibernating bats was trapped when an old mine was capped, but quick action by state officials reopened the mine and saved the bats.

At a time when conservationists and industry officials rarely agree on anything, these stories must be told. Bats are too valuable to lose, if only because they eat so many flying insects. A single little brown bat can eat up to 600 mosquitoes per hour. Therefore, a colony of just 10 bats eats thousands of insects each night. The 20 million bats that roost in Texas's Bracken Cave eat 250 tons of insects every night!

So if ever a bat gets loose in your house, stay calm and count your blessings. It simply means your natural bug zapper is on duty.

(If you know of any bridges or mines used by roosting or hibernating bats, contact Bat Conservation International, P.O. Box 162603, Austin, Texas 78716.)

## *Meadow Voles & Kestrels* 2/9/97 (4/95)

In the hayfield near my house lives an abundant small vertebrate whose population sometimes exceeds 200 per acre. But I rarely see one. Usually they stay hidden under the tunnels of grass they build just above the surface of the ground.

Meadow voles. Out of sight, out of mind. Few people see them and most probably don't even know they exist. Yet they are the keystone species in any grassland ecosystem. Remove them, and a complicated food web would collapse. Predators, from snakes and weasels to foxes and hawks, would go hungry.

Meadow voles are often called field mice or meadow mice, though they hardly resemble mice. Compared to a cute little deer mouse, meadow voles are two to three times heavier, they have beady black eyes and their ears are short and concealed by fur. If you have a cat that deposits its kills on your doorstep, the description should sound familiar.

Aptly named, meadow voles inhabit ungrazed meadows and fields. They require the layer of thatch that covers the ground. Here they construct complex patterns of inch-wide tunnels that allow them to move about unseen from above.

47

During the winter they escape the cold in underground burrows. They build globular grassy nests both underground and inside dense tufts of grass.

In these nests, meadow voles do what they do best -- have babies. Weather permitting, they breed year 'round. Gestation lasts just 21 days, and the five to eight babies grow rapidly. Young voles wean in two weeks and are independent one week later. Young males breed at five weeks of age; females are sexually mature at four weeks. This reproductive prowess explains how one captive female produced 17 litters in just one year, and one of her daughters had 13 litters before reaching her first birthday.

Though meadow voles reproduce rapidly they do not maintain stable populations. Their numbers peak and crash on a four year cycle. From highs of more than 200 per acre, they can almost disappear before rebounding to abundance. Cyclic populations would seem to be problematic for predators. Most predators, however, simply switch to other prey that are more common when vole numbers are down.

Erriki Korpimaki, a visiting zoologist at the University of British Columbia, wondered how European kestrels (a small falcon, similar to our American kestrel) cope with unpredictable numbers of voles, a favorite food. He noticed that when kestrels returned to Scandinavia each spring, they did not always return to the exact same place. Yet they almost unerringly established their territories in places where voles numbers were high. He wondered how they did it.

A recent report in *Discover* magazine explains Korpimaki's answer. He discovered that vole runways are visible in ultraviolet light and that kestrels can see u-v light. Because voles mark their trails with urine and feces, which just happen to absorb u-v light, Korpimaki suspected there might be a connection.

In laboratory tests he discovered that kestrels ignored unmarked trails illuminated by either light source, they ignored marked trails illuminated by normal visible light, but they overwhelmingly preferred marked trails illuminated by u-v light. Follow-up field tests confirmed that kestrels seek out excreta-marked vole trails in nature.

When kestrels return each spring, they apparently search the ground below for the tell-tale dark steaks left behind by fresh vole urine and feces. It's a fascinating variation on the old "where there's smoke, there's fire" maxim.

It hardly seems fair. Not only are voles eaten by virtually every predator that roams their habitat, they are even pursued by aerial hunters equipped with radar-like technology. If we apply the European example to all vole-kestrel interactions, perhaps erratic population cycles are voles' answer to intense kestrel predation. If vole numbers vary from year to year and place to place, a single predator cannot become vole-dependent.

## *Muskrats & Marshes*                    (1/90)

A marsh in winter is a quiet place. No colonies of red-winged blackbirds nesting in the cattails. No bullfrogs bellowing from the water's edge. No mosquitoes buzzing in your ear. No turtles basking in the sun, ready to drop loudly into the water when you venture too closely.

And if the water freezes, even ducks, geese and herons abandon the marsh for open water farther south.

In mid-winter a marsh seems a dead zone. And on the surface it is. But beneath the ice, fish swim (albeit less enthusiastically than they do in warmer weather) and muskrats go about their business of managing the marsh.

No animal is more important to a marsh than the muskrat. The collective appetite of the entire muskrat population determines how much of the marsh will remain open water and how much will be overgrown with cattails, bulrushes and water lilies. Muskrats eat these and other aquatic plants.

When the muskrat population is low, aquatic plants prosper and take over the marsh. Open water disappears. When muskrat populations rebound and climb, they reduce the abundance of aquatic plants and create more open water.

It's one of many natural life cycles. More muskrats eat more food. Soon there's not enough food to feed all the muskrats so they starve or move out, and the population declines. While the muskrat population bottoms out, aquatic

49

vegetation rebounds. The increased food supply triggers population growth among the muskrats and their numbers increase. More muskrats eat more food..... And so it goes.

The consequences of all this extend far beyond muskrats and aquatic plants. Marshes act as natural sponges that filter pollutants from surface water and make it safe for human use. (That's why conservationists are always screaming, "Save wetlands! Don't drain! Don't develop them!")

When a muskrat population explodes, it can denude a marsh quickly. A denuded marsh becomes a stagnant mud hole with little filtering ability. Consequently the quality of our surface water suffers. Muskrats affect people.

The open water muskrats create and maintain attracts shorebirds, wading birds, ducks and many species of song birds. The aquatic vegetation that remains provides cover for fish, broods of ducklings and adult ducks rendered flightless by their annual molt. Some ducks and geese build their nests on top of muskrat houses. Muskrats affect other wildlife.

If only there was a way to manipulate muskrat populations so a marsh could be stabilized to consist of about half open water and half vegetation. Such a tool exists. It's called trapping. I know trapping and the fur industry are under fire these days, but hear me out.

As a kid, I had no trouble justifying trapping on moral, economic or recreational grounds. It got me outside, and it kept a few bucks in my pocket. It was money that I used to buy the field guides and animal books that helped lead me to a career as a conservationist.

As an adult, however, I have a real problem justifying trapping on moral, economic or recreational grounds. I can, however, and I have in the first two-thirds of this essay, justified trapping ecologically.

We must manage marshes to stabilize them so they can do their job of purifying surface water and providing habitat for many other wild creatures. The easiest and cheapest way to manage marshes is to trap muskrats. Trapping muskrats is the ideal solution because they breed prolifically and have voracious appetites for aquatic vegetation.

My yardstick for evaluating any management tool is, "Can I justify it ecologically?" If the answer is yes, and there are people, for what ever reason, willing to do the job, then use the tool.

As the sun slipped below the horizon, the woods grew dark quickly. Off to my left, a flash of white caught my eye. It moved purposefully, expertly maneuvering right and left to avoid the tree trunks that blocked its flight path. It landed about six feet above the ground on the trunk of a large white oak. Instantly, the flying squirrel scurried to the far side of the trunk, as if shaking an owl in hot pursuit.

Southern flying squirrels (*Glaucomys volans*, which literally means" little flying mouse") inhabit most deciduous and mixed deciduous/coniferous woods east of the Great Plains. Their nocturnal nature, however, relegates them to seldom seen, unfamiliar status. That's only because most of us spend little time in the woods after dark. An evening in any woodlot, especially one dominated by oaks or beeches, is one way to remedy this situation.

Listen for the sound of teeth gnawing nuts overhead or watch for flashes of white gliding from tree to tree. As a flying squirrel twists and turns through the forest's obstacle course of outstretched branches, its white belly stands out in the darkening woods. When it lands, note how it disappears to the back of the tree, a habit that no doubt pays off on those evenings when it crosses paths with a hungry owl. As soon as the coast is judged clear, the flying squirrel reappears to go about its business.

In February it might visit a bird feeder, eat swollen buds or slice into the bark of a sugar maple and lap up the sap that flows. In May it switches to insects and occasionally raids bird nests for a meal of fresh eggs or nestlings. In August mushrooms, fruits, berries and mice are abundant and irresistible. And in October the prudent flying squirrel gathers and stores bushels of acorns, beechnuts, walnuts and hickory nuts to get them through the coming winter. Fairy diddles, as flying squirrels are often called, eat whatever the forest provides.

By day, flying squirrels sleep in tree cavities, often in groups of four to 12 individuals during the winter. Flying squirrels do not hibernate; they huddle together in small groups to stay warm.

After breeding in February or March, females live the life of a single mother. By now most adult females are bred and waiting out their 40-day pregnancy. Three or four pups are born in April or May in a tree cavity. (I often find at least one flying squirrel nursery in the nest boxes I maintain around my house.) The young are weaned in about five weeks. They stay with their mother until her second litter is born in July or August.

By the time the pups are seven weeks old, they are almost as large as their mother and ready to test their "wings." Of course, flying squirrels do not fly. They glide from the tree to tree or to the ground courtesy of a flap of skin that runs from wrist to ankle on each side of the body. Upon takeoff, this skin balloons and permits a controlled glide from tree to tree. The tail serves as a rudder to guide the "flight." Most flights are short, 30 to 40 feet, but biologists have observed flights up to 300 feet.

Flying squirrels have always ranked as one of my favorite animals. Their big black eyes and silky soft fur endear them to anyone who encounters them -- unless they're living in your attic. Flying squirrels can be noisy, and their nightly antics make sleep difficult. Live-trap and remove them before the first litter is born, or the problem will worsen. And unless you seal all entry holes to the attic, they'll be back.

## *Acorns & Squirrels* (10/93)

When a red-tailed hawk chases a cottontail, the rabbit hightails it to the nearest thicket. When a largemouth bass attacks a crayfish, the crayfish darts to the nearest burrow. And when a black rat snake stalks a deer mouse, the mouse relies on vigilance and quickness to elude the snake's deadly coils. These predator/prey interactions are familiar to even armchair naturalists.

But what of plants? Is it possible for plants to escape the jaws of a hungry herbivore? Surprisingly, the answer is yes.

Some plants, such as roses, raspberries and cacti, arm themselves with thorns. Others, such as milkweeds and locoweed, produce toxic chemicals that poison animals naive enough to eat them. And in the tropics some species of acacia "permit" ants to live inside their thorns and drink their nectar. In return, the ants attack anything that so much as brushes against their host trees.

But one of the most fascinating botanical anti-predator strategies takes place in our own backyards. Acorns are an abundant, widespread and nutritious food. Every fall squirrels scurry around the forest floor in search of acorns, which they gather and cache in shallow underground middens. At first glance, it seems unlikely that acorns could in any way defend themselves. But they do.

First, we need to understand that oaks are classified into two basic groups: the white oaks and the red oaks. Among the differences between the two groups of oaks is the timing of acorn germination.

Red oak acorns, like most temperate plants, lie dormant on the forest floor all winter long and germinate in the spring. Squirrels gather these acorns each fall and store them throughout the woods. In so doing, squirrels act as dispersal agents, ensuring that red oaks get distributed around the forest. They also plant the seeds in suitable fertile soil. Because squirrels never retrieve all their hidden food, forgotten acorns germinate a new generation of red oaks.

Many species of white oaks, on the other hand, germinate soon after they fall to the ground. This adaptation enables white oaks to escape the jaws of squirrels. White oak taproots grow rapidly in the fall and serves as the winter food storage organ. By transferring much of the energy that was in the acorn to the underground taproot, white oaks escape predation by squirrels.

Gray squirrels, however, have learned to beat the white oaks at their own game. Adult gray squirrels can somehow distinguish between red and white oaks (perhaps by smell, taste or feel). When they find a white oak acorn, they kill it by notching the nut with their sharp incisors and cutting out the embryo. Then the squirrel buries it. A notched acorn is incapable of germinating, but the meat of the nut remains nutritious until the squirrel retrieves it during the winter.

If this system were perfect, white oaks would be rare. Instead, they are among the most common trees in the eastern deciduous forest. That's because this acorn killing strategy is a learned behavior. It takes time for young squirrels to learn it, so there are always white oak acorns that escape, survive and germinate. In fact, squirrels notch fewer than half of all the white oak acorns they cache.

Just as animal predators and prey engage in a never ending battle of attack and counterattack, plants also engage in a continual struggle to survive. Botanical anti-predator strategies may be subtle, but they are as effective as any practiced by animals. Note that the operative word is "effective," not "perfect." In nature, perfection isn't required. Adaptive behaviors must work only often enough to ensure that plants and animals achieve life's ultimate goal -- successful reproduction.

## *Coyotes* (2/95)

Travel an interstate in almost any western state and sooner or later you will see a coyote. It's a symbol of the west, admired by some, vilified by many. Ranchers in particular hate coyotes because they have acquired a taste for slow, stupid prey -- livestock.

For decades the U.S. Department of Agriculture has waged a war against the coyote. Using guns, traps and poisons, government-sponsored programs kill tens of thousands of coyotes annually. Yet coyotes thrive. In fact, there are probably more coyotes roaming the west today than there were 50 years ago.

One reason coyotes seem unfazed by control efforts is that they don't mind neighbors. They learn to stay out of rifle range, they become trap-shy, and they adapt well to suburban life. As people populate the plains and deserts, coyotes learn they are relatively safe in populated areas, and they learn to eat another easy to kill prey -- pets.

Over the last 50 years, coyotes have expanded their range eastward. They can now be found in virtually every state east of the Mississippi River -- and not uncommonly. In

Pennsylvania, for example, coyotes occur in every county, including Philadelphia.

Unfortunately, eastern coyotes enjoy the same reputation as their western cousins. They eat sheep, dogs and cats. Some hunters even fear they control some game populations. So control programs have followed coyotes east.

I'm in the minority. I like coyotes; always have. I saw my first one along an interstate in west Texas back in the mid 1970s when I moved to Arizona for graduate school. They were common in the high desert of northern Arizona. Years later, while living in Oklahoma, I'd see them whenever I traveled from Stillwater to Oklahoma City or Tulsa. But they were wary. They always stayed far from the highway. Control has succeeded only in breeding a race of super-wily coyotes. They trust nothing associated with man.

One reason coyotes thrive in the face of government's campaign to eradicate them is their reproductive response to declining populations. Unlike many animals, which disappear quickly when a population reaches a certain lower threshold, coyotes increase their reproductive rate as their population declines.

Coyotes average six pups per litter, but when populations are low, litter size jumps to seven. When population rebound to normal levels, litter size drops to four. Food supply also affects reproduction. When prey is abundant, coyotes make more babies. Hence, coyotes prosper.

Interesting natural history, you say, but what good are they? Are coyotes not just varmints worthy of scorn? A recent paper in the *Journal of Wildlife Management* suggests that coyotes are far more than a predator that simply keeps prey populations in check.

Biologists in North Dakota suggest that the presence of coyotes actually increases the nesting success of ducks. The northern prairies of North America produce most of the continent's waterfowl. Unfortunately predation, mostly by red foxes, keeps nest success low. Where red foxes were common, duck nest success was only 17 percent. Where coyotes were common, duck nest success almost doubled to 32 percent.

Coyotes do not tolerate foxes. Whether they drive them out of an area or actually kill them is unclear. The practical result, however, is that where coyotes occur red fox population numbers decline. This is great news for duck enthusiasts. Red foxes love duck eggs, coyotes do not. So when coyotes dominate an area, duck nest success increases.

The lesson here is a familiar one. Predators are important, not only by controlling prey, but also by maintaining structure among animal communities. Just because we don't yet understand a species' value, does not mean it has no value. It only highlights our ignorance.

Too often, we take the easy way out. Coyotes kill sheep, so we kill coyotes, regardless of the consequences. Tunnel vision breeds ignorance. Research breeds knowledge and understanding. This is why we value science.

## *Feral Cats* (4/96)

I could just make out the rear end of the black-and-white cat in the weeds along the edge of the road. It belonged to no one and was as wild as any raccoon or fox. I stopped and watched from about 25 yards away. For eight minutes the cat crouched motionless. If my kids had been along, I'm sure I could have convinced them the cat was stuffed.

Suddenly, the cat twitched its butt, a sign that an attack was imminent. A few seconds later, the cat's powerful hind legs uncoiled, and it pounced into denser vegetation. Moments later, the hunter returned to the road with a lifeless cardinal in its mouth. It trotted contentedly toward an old abandoned truck in a neighbor's pasture.

I'm sure I could see a similar drama along the roads near my rural home every day. Feral cats are everywhere. And their impact on wildlife populations is only beginning to be understood.

A feral cat is an escapee, a refugee from domestication. Unwanted, abandoned house cats readily adapt to the wild. Shelter is abundant. Abandoned buildings, barns, brush piles, culvert pipes, and even junk cars are just a few of the places feral cats call home. And food is often equally abundant.

Feral cats eat chipmunks, mice, rabbits, birds, roadkills, garbage and food intended for house pets.

Though I admire feral cats' adaptability, I object to their diet. Throughout winter they visit bird feeders regularly for easy meals. Nothing annoys me more than to see a big old tom wander up the hill just after I find a bloody pile of yellow and black feathers under one of my feeders. And in the spring and summer feral cats destroy countless nests of song birds, grouse, turkeys, cottontails, chipmunks and squirrels.

Some might counter that feral cats also eat their fair share of rats and mice. That's true, and it's no doubt a reason many farmers tolerate feral cats. But this only fuels my argument. Every rodent a feral cat eats is one less meal for hawks, owls, snakes and other predators. Anyway you look at it, feral cats are bad news.

And it's not an insignificant problem. Estimates of the U.S. feral cat population range from 10 to 30 million. That's in addition to 60 million pet cats in America. The impact of feral felines on populations of song birds and small mammals must be staggering.

Let's consider a very conservative example. Assume there are only 10 million feral cats in the U.S. Now assume further that each of these cats kills just two song birds or small mammals each week. That's more than one billion birds and mammals annually. It is certainly not unreasonable to suggest that feral cats might be partly responsible for the declining North American song bird populations.

One solution to the growing feral cat problem is to neuter pet cats before they breed. Ideally, every pet cat should be neutered. (Yes, mine is.) A single female can bear two to 10 kittens three times per year when food and shelter are available. That means one unwanted female cat can produce as many as 30 kittens within a year, not to mention the "grandchildren" her daughters will bear before that year is up. Such reproductive potential dramatizes the importance of controlling pet populations as one way to slow the increase in feral cat numbers.

The solution to the existing feral cat problem is more complicated. Left unchecked, their population will continue to grow. Declaring an open season on feral cats might seem a reasonable response to some, but that would almost certainly create myriad legal, ethical and moral problems. Perhaps a more responsible solution would be to live-trap the cats, take them to an animal shelter and let professionals dispose of them.

Feral cats are efficient and brutal predators. They hunt and kill even when they are well fed. The responsibility for the ecological havoc they wreak, however, lies not with the cats, but with people who abandon them.

## *White-Tailed Deer* (11/95)

Nature appeals to everyone. On television specials, for example, who can resist the allure of African lions and elephants, Brazilian jungle cats or arctic polar bears? And just last week the discovery in Madagascar of a tiny primate, long thought to be extinct, made headlines around the world.

But our intense interest in these exotic species is short-lived. The principle of "out of sight, out of mind" applies. It takes common, everyday events to kindle long-term, unwavering interest.

Consider, for example, white-tailed deer. Here in Marshall County, West Virginia deer roam every ridge and valley. It's a rare six-mile trip to town that I don't see at least a few, and at dawn or dusk I often count herds of 20 or 30. Yet, common as they are, I always watch and wonder. And so do many other local residents.

Just yesterday I was following a neighbor into town. I was in a bit of a hurry -- I had to get to the post office before it closed. Suddenly his car slowed to about 10 mph, and I noticed him staring off into the field. The object of his attention? A herd of 11 deer.

Now, this man is old enough to be retired and has hunted deer since he was a boy. So what was the fascination? His answer, "I just like to watch 'em," offers little insight.

Perhaps he was dreaming of next fall. Or perhaps he remembered last fall or even his first hunt.

Whatever the appeal, it's relentless. I yield to it, too. During the only snow of consequence during this mild winter, a doe and her two yearlings began visiting my backyard bird feeders. They cleaned the ground of spilled sunflower seeds and sometimes licked my tray feeder empty. I put out whole corn for them, and they visited two or three times a day.

This shouldn't be a big deal for me. I see deer every day. But when they stand in my yard just 20 feet from my desk, I can't resist. I watch. As long as they let me.

I study the luxurious coat and notice details I never see at a distance -- a white throat, the swollen lumps that soon will support a set of antlers, black fur surrounding the black, fleshy nose.

I admire their vigilance. Any unexpected movement or sound puts them on alert. Heads jerk. Ears cock. Feet stamp the earth. The leader snorts defiantly, then flees, waving its white flag in warning, not surrender, to the rest of the herd.

When I try to analyze this fascination, I come up with a number of possible explanations. Perhaps we love deer because we admire how they thrive amidst the havoc we've wreaked upon the planet. They bring a sense of wildness and adventure into an otherwise tame and predictable world.

Or perhaps we appreciate what we once did not have. Thirty years ago deer were not common. In fact, in this part of West Virginia, they were actually rare. Long time residents report that seeing a deer in the 1950s was an event. And word of the news traveled fast. So now when a local sees deer, he remembers the old days and appreciates at least one change the '80s has wrought.

But maybe I'm overanalyzing. Perhaps it's enough to just enjoy wild things. My five-year old daughter explains the appeal of deer quite simply -- "I love their big brown eyes." I can't argue with that.

# Part 2

# Purely Personal

## Why I Write

I love wild things. That's why I write this column. I try to make nature less puzzling and frightening and more exciting and wondrous.

My first such efforts were as a university professor, where I taught 200 to 300 students each year. But I left academia six years ago because I realized that over the course of a 30-year career, I'd have direct contact with fewer than 10,000 students. Sure, many of them would go on to become teachers or conservation volunteers and my indirect effect would be much greater, but I wanted to have a more immediate impact.

So I shifted gears and began writing for general audiences. Each week this column reaches 100 times more readers than the number of students I would have taught in an entire academic career. And based on your letters, I can claim at least a small measure of success.

For example, Rosie Noll of Jackson Center, Pa. writes, "I always feel like you are speaking just to me. You wrote about keeping nature notes, and I started a journal. I saw my first Blackburnian warbler, and you wrote about warblers. I got interested in bats and you wrote about them.

"I get such pleasure reading my journal and reliving the wonderful times I've had in the woods. It's gotten to where I can't wait to get back to the beaver swamp (that's where I do most of my birding).

"Then you wrote what was for me the most important article ever -- plans for bluebird houses. Building bird houses had been a goal of mine for years, but I had no tools or know-how.

"I showed my husband the plans and asked if he could teach me how to build them. He said, 'Sure. This is easy!' And it was. We build them every winter, and this year we got the whole neighborhood involved.

"And I give some as gifts to friends. It's so great to have a friend say, 'I never knew a bird could be so blue.' Other friends copied the plans and built their own.

"But here's the real reason I wrote. This afternoon (October 7) I opened a bluebird box just for the heck of it. I saw a nest of leaves.

"At first I thought -- deer mice, so I called my husband and daughter to come see the nest. With a stick I gently pulled down the top of the nest. Suddenly a smooth, round shape and a large, dark eye appeared. I quickly shut the box and informed my family that we had a flying squirrel. Another dream realized.

"Now I'm really excited! I'm ready to try screech-owl, kestrel, wood duck and bat houses!

"A few years ago, I had never even seen a bluebird. Now I'm known locally as the 'bird lady' and people call me for advice. And it all started with you. Keep up the good work!"

I felt great when I read Rosie's letter. It makes the time and expense of sending out more than 3,000 copies of nest box plans and hundreds of other letters worthwhile.

I share this with you not to pat myself on the back, but to remind you why I write this column and to thank you for your feedback. This forum is as much yours as mine. Keep those cards and letters coming.

## Chasing Dreams                                    (7/94)

*SS Opening 10-26-97*

The end of summer is a time to reflect. Vacation's over. It's back to work and back to school.

Twenty years ago I had a brand new diploma from the University of Delaware and was looking forward to graduate school at Northern Arizona University in Flagstaff. My dream was to live "out west."

So in August, 1974 I overloaded my tiny Plymouth Cricket and began a journey that continues even today. I spent the first night on the road camped by a stream in Virginia's Jefferson National Forest. I was sure I'd encounter a bear that night. I didn't, but the dream had begun.

The next morning I hopped on I-40 and headed west. I remember seeing coyotes and scissor-tailed flycatchers in Oklahoma, prairie dogs and burrowing owls in the Texas panhandle and pronghorn, magpies and scrub jays in New Mexico.

When I arrived in Flagstaff, I set up camp in the Coconino National Forest just north of town. The ponderosa pines that dominated the forest were new to me. But the wind whistled softly through the pines and bid me welcome. Even as I write this, I can smell the sweet vanilla scent of the ponderosa's aromatic bark. Stellar's jays, the western ecological equivalent of our blue jay, provided the loud raucous background music for my first Arizona lunch. Overhead, a family of pygmy nuthatches foraged in the branches. My fingers grew weary from constantly paging through field guides. I had discovered a whole new world.

After devoting a few days to find a place to live and register for classes, I took off to explore the southwest. I had arrived several weeks early, so I had plenty of time.

The first stop was the Grand Canyon. When I first saw that hole on the earth, my jaw dropped. I couldn't believe it. It remains the most wondrous sight I've ever seen. Words cannot do it justice, so I won't even try. Just trust me, and see it for yourself someday.

Over the course of the next several weeks I visited most of the national parks and monuments in the four corners area of Arizona, Utah, Colorado and New Mexico. I remember seeing my first golden eagle standing on the desert floor near Shiprock, New Mexico. I remember the fantasyland called Bryce Canyon -- arguably God's best effort at building sand castles. I remember sleeping under the stars at Arches National Park. But I didn't sleep. All night long I watched shooting stars streak across the pitch black sky. Later I was almost disappointed to learn that I had caught the peak of the Perseids meteor shower. I thought I had somehow peeked into heaven.

For 20 years I've been chasing dreams. One summer my wife and I traveled from Michigan to Washington on U.S. Route 2 -- 5,000 miles in 17 days. We saw Mt. St. Helen's before she blew her stack. For four years I led birding tours to Mexico, where the tiny western state of Colima came to feel like a second home, and its people like family. I've traveled to Alaska, caught dozens of salmon and seen Kodiak brown bears, killer whales and sea otters. This summer I took my family to Maine, where we watched whales and moose.

The dream chase continues. I'm planning a trip to the Galapagos Islands -- home of giant tortoises, marine iguanas, Darwin's finches and the birthplace of Charles Darwin's thoughts on the origins of species. It is the one place on earth every biologist yearns to visit.

Dreams make life worth living. My only regret is that one lifetime is too short to realize them all.

## *October Lessons* (10/93)

October, like no other month, speaks to me. It calls me outdoors. It demands I set aside time to roam the woods with my wife and daughters.

I guess its pay back time. Years ago my dad took me for long walks on crisp October Sundays. He said we were going to collect hickory nuts. He stockpiled them so he could snack on cold winter nights. As I look back, though, I suspect (or maybe hope) this was just his way of spending some time with me.

We'd walk the dirt roads near our rural home. He taught me to recognize those trees he knew -- hickories, walnuts, oaks, sassafras, maples. He'd marvel at the predictable synchrony of the fall colors. Sumac and Virginia creeper always turned first. His favorites, the bright red sassafras and dogwoods, brightened our October outings. By Thanksgiving, oaks and hickories had closed out the show.

If he was still here I could explain that the timing of nature's fall festival is set by day length and fine tuned by temperature. I'd explain how each species' biological clock responds uniquely to autumn's progressively shorter days. At the appointed time chlorophyll, the pigment that makes plants green, breaks down and lets other pigments express themselves. The yellows, reds, oranges and browns. That's why we see the same pattern every year, I'd tell him.

We'd study the grand old snags -- skeletons of once massive trees -- and marvel how life teemed in a body that had been for decades dead. A red-tailed hawk perched on the highest branch and scanned the field below for a cocky cottontail.

From a lower branch, a phoebe sallied back and forth after the few remaining flying insects. Months earlier, in June, we had watched a kestrel carry a mouse to its nest in an old woodpecker hole.

Yet, as much as he enjoyed the theater in the snag, he couldn't help but wonder why someone didn't cut it down for firewood.

If he was still here, I'd explain how ecology had finally caught up to his gut-level appreciation of those old dead trees. We now understand that trees live on for decades after they die. Insects invade the bark. Woodpeckers eat the insects and excavate nest cavities. Then other cavity-dwellers -- screech-owls, kestrels, bluebirds, rat snakes, tree frogs, spiders -- move in. Indigo buntings sing and eastern phoebes hunt from the exposed branches. Eventually the tree rots, crumbles, falls... and returns its nutrients to the soil for a new generation of plants.

But he's not here. He's been gone for 15 Octobers now. So I take my daughters to the woods and teach them what I know, just as I have taken my grandchildern.

I explain how shorter fall days trigger the biological clocks of trees, insects, box turtles, chipmunks, geese and other migratory birds. I explain that photoperiod is the only absolutely reliable clock to which plants and animals can set their own. It's an unerring standard. Year after year, millennium after millennium, autumn days grow shorter as winter approaches. Trees drop their leaves, birds head south and other animals fatten themselves for the winter. Come spring, the days grow longer. The cycle of life begins anew. Without fail.

We study snags and the life that abounds in them. They understand why I never cut a snag for firewood. They understand why I sometimes intentionally girdle a healthy tree to create a new snag. And they understand how my nest boxes help make up for too few natural cavities.

We collect nuts, too. Hickory nuts, acorns, walnuts. We take them home, dry them and save them for winter. But we don't eat them all ourselves. On frosty winter mornings we crack a few as we sip hot chocolate and put them out for woodpeckers, nuthatches, titmice, chickadees and blue jays. I explain that these birds enjoy nut meats as much as we enjoy a venison tenderloin.

Yes, October speaks to me. It tells me to teach my children, just as my father taught me. Nothing in this life brings me greater pleasure.

## *A Cosmic Perspective* (8/92)

The night before the July new moon was dark, cool and clear -- ideal conditions to catch a shooting star. At 10 o'clock we left the house and hiked up to the hayfield, one of the highest points in the county.

Nora, 8 at the time, was excited and looking forward to seeing a natural fireworks display. Emma, almost 3, was less enthusiastic. She couldn't understand why we going for a walk when she should be sound asleep. But as long as she was with her mom and sister, she decided it was OK.

We carried flashlights and a blanket, and our dog and three cats followed at our heels. I'm sure they, too, couldn't quite figure out what was going on. When we reached the top of the hill, I spread the blanket, and we laid down on our backs to wait for the show to begin. We had hardly gotten comfortable when the first "star" burned a trail across the sky. Nora squealed with delight. Linda and I "oo"-ed and "ah"-ed. Emma missed it.

About six minutes later another meteor lit the sky. This one burned much brighter than the first, and the trail lingered for several seconds. Emma missed it. Over the course of the next hour, we counted eight shooting stars. We probably missed again as many as our collective concentration ebbed and flowed. Emma missed them all. I think she still wonders what we did that night.

Occasional shooting stars can be seen at any time of year, but July and August are the best times to catch meteor showers, which are named for the constellations they appear to originate from. Meteors, most are specks of stone or iron the size sand grains, burn up in the earth's atmosphere and, of course, are no where near the stars. Those that do make it through the atmosphere and land are called meteorites.

For a experience you'll never forget, make time to watch the night sky. Get away from city lights and spend a night under the stars. The best time to see shooting stars is after midnight. The best place is in the country, away from the glare of city lights.

In between the shooting stars, which will flash by briefly every few minutes, find the Big Dipper. Extend a line from the two stars of the bowl farthest from the handle. About five times the distance between these two pointers stars, beyond the top of the bowl, you'll find Polaris, the north star. Nearby, Cassiopeia's "W" hangs low in the north sky.

After your eyes acclimate to the darkness, you'll notice a massive, pale apparition crossing the heavens. It's the Milky Way Galaxy, our cosmic home. The Earth, the sun and our entire solar system are part of the Milky Way. As you gaze upon the Milky Way, exercise your mind. It contains about one trillion stars, measures 500,000 light-years across and is 12 billion years old. (A light-year is the distance light, which travels 186,000 miles per second, travels in one year). And then note that the Milky Way is just one of millions of galaxies in the universe.

On a clear, dark night you can sense the cosmos and put humanity into perspective. In nature's grand scheme we're all as important as a mite on a hair on a leg of flea on a dog. It's a lesson in humility that we all need once in while.

# *Swimming Holes* (6/91)

We called it "The Rock." It is where my father taught my brothers and me to swim. But the name misleads. Debris from an ancient ice age, many rocks, including some house-sized boulders, ringed our favorite swimming hole.

From the largest boulders, we learned to dive into the deep, spring-fed pool below. After the day's first dive, we surfaced and screamed. Even Pop would let out a "whoop" when he came up and shook the water off his face. The water at "The Rock" was always cold. We called it refreshing.

Every day during summer vacation, I'd wait for my dad to come home from work. "Can we go swimming?" I'd plead before he even got out of the car. More often than not, we went. After a long day in a hot die-casting factory, Pop was usually more anxious than any of us to cool off.

Sometimes we'd just take a "dip." We stayed in the water only long enough to chill our bodies to the bone. But when we toweled off to leave, we all smelled clean and fresh.

More often we'd eat an early supper and spend the entire evening swimming. And while town kids spent Saturday and Sunday afternoons at the city pool, we went to "The Rock."

After the initial shock that came with that first dive into the frigid swimming hole, the water seemed to get warmer. It didn't. Our bodies merely acclimated to the cold. Of course, it didn't hurt that we never stopped moving. That was the only way to ward off the goose bumps. Swimming, climbing, jumping, diving. We played as hard and as recklessly as my kids do now, 30 years later.

But as I look back, it was more than just simple fun. I learned a lot, too. In between all the swimming and diving, I'd rest in the shallows or climb upstream through the riffles and rapids. I'd flip rocks and find new and exciting creatures.

When I got home, I'd thumb through my dog-eared field guides. I learned about the life cycles of aquatic insects by identifying the larval stages of dragonflies, stoneflies, mayflies and Dobsonflies. And I met some fascinating adults, too -- water boatmen, backswimmers and giant water bugs.

My favorite critters were crayfish, mussels and fish. I loved the way crayfish propelled themselves backwards to escape my grasp. I learned quickly how to hold the big ones by their shells so they couldn't pinch me and bring tears. I remember discovering freshwater mussels -- a lesson that all clams don't live in the ocean. And with the aid of a mask, I swam with the fishes and learned to recognize them -- darters, chubs, shiners, sunfish, bass and trout.

My memories of "The Rock" are vivid and precious. It was fun family time. That's why I was so excited when some friends invited my wife to bring the kids and me to their special swimming hole not far from our ridge-top home.

Because, you see, a swimming hole isn't something you just find and claim. It belongs to the regulars. And one becomes a regular by invitation only.

Now my family has a swimming hole. A place where we can splash, jump, dive, refresh and explore on a sizzling summer day. When I watch my girls, I remember my dad diving off the highest rock, brother Alex dunking brother Michael under water for the umpteenth time and mom shivering in the shallows.

I pity kids who have never swum anywhere but a city pool. They grow up thinking all water comes from a spigot and reeks of chlorine. That all water is clear, sterile, lifeless and luke warm. They'll never know "The Rock" or any place like it. And they'll be poorer for it.

So if ever a country friend invites you for a dip at their favorite swimming hole, go. May minnows nibble your knees, crawdads pinch your toes and your skin tingle as it never has before.

### *Blackberry Season* (7/91)

We dress for battle: leather boots, old jeans, socks pulled up over our pant-legs, a long-sleeved shirt, and an old baseball cap. Add a small bucket and a machete, and we're fully armed. Blackberries, here we come.

If you've never picked blackberries, you have no idea what an ordeal it is. Searing heat, steamy humidity, nagging gnats, stinging bees, biting horse flies, sharp thorns, poison ivy, and ticks top the list of natural wonders you'll encounter. Add two whining children and an occasional black snake that startles you silly, and you have a pretty good picture of the whole process.

But each summer, my whole family eagerly goes forth into battle. And so do many friends and neighbors. The rewards are sweet: quarts and sometimes even gallons of plump, purple fruits that we eat over cereal or ice cream, cook up into batches of jam, or bake into cakes and cobblers. One of nature's finest "freebies," my wife claims.

Animals love blackberries, too. Purple bird droppings stain leaves, branches, fences and clothes on the washline. Deer trails crisscross our favorite patches. And mammal scats sprinkled with tiny, telltale yellow seeds (like those that stick in our teeth) hint at the competition we face. More than 100 species of birds and mammals feast on blackberries and the fruits of other brambles, such as raspberries and dewberries.

Blackberries thrive in areas disturbed by humans -- old fields, pastures, utility rights-of-way, roadsides and fencerows. They're just another example of the enormous potential these areas hold for wildlife if we don't poison them with herbicides or keep them closely mowed and "clean."

Blackberries and other brambles belong to the genus *Rubus*. This genus provides more food for wildlife than any other shrub on the continent. Not only do animals eat the fruits, but some browsers also eat the leaves and stems.

The value to wildlife doesn't stop there. Brambles form dense thickets, providing excellent escape cover and nesting habitat for birds and small mammals. These thickets are often so dense we either use the machete to hack our way to the center or settle for working the perimeter.

Slender, thorny canes characterize brambles, including blackberries. The stems can be upright or trailing. Short-lived, they produce fruit only in their second year, then die back to be replaced by new stems. But when they touch the ground, tips of blackberry canes send out new roots, which give rise to new canes. (These arching stems rooted at both ends are one reason bramble thickets are so impenetrable.) Furthermore, bramble root systems are perennial, so even though individual canes are short-lived, a thicket can persist for many years.

The stems are covered with oval-shaped leaflets in groups of three or five. So beware: these leaflets often look similar to and tend to mask poison ivy, which typically thrives in the same locations. Most berry pickers eventually learn this lesson the hard way.

Many people confuse blackberries with black raspberries due to the similar color of their fruits. But their are several clues that reveal their true identities.

For example, the color and shape of their canes. Black raspberries have round stems covered with a white, powdery film. (The "powder" actually rubs off on your finger.) Blackberries stems, on the other hand, are green and ridged -- almost square in cross-section.

The fruits, though virtually identical in appearance, differ in how they cling to the stem. Raspberries slide easily from a small, spongy cone, leaving a small "cup" on the fruit. They fall off the plant when ripe, even if undisturbed. Blackberries must be plucked from the stem and have no "cup." And ripened blackberries dry and shrivel on the stem if not harvested.

But not too many have a chance to shrivel up around here. We see to that.


## Grasses   ss Group Opening 4-6-97   (8/91)

To most of us, grass is an aesthetically pleasing yard ornament that requires constant attention -- mow, water, mow, fertilize, mow...

Several years ago I spent four weeks in North Dakota. I came home with a new appreciation for the grasses. So did my daughter, Nora, who was nine years old at the time. She kept an journal and wrote, in part, "The grass seems to talk to us. It wants to say hello. But we cut it down. The grass hides things that need to be hidden. But we cut it down. One day the grass will hide us."

My reaction to the endless prairie was equally stirring. Grasses grow. Breezes blow. Rivers flow. Hills roll. Wildflowers wave. Bobolinks sing. Bison graze. And distant horizons go on forever.

The prairie images dim as time passes, but they brighten every time I fire up the backyard grill. A bed of glowing coals cradles a dozen ears of sweet corn, steaming in their husks. A steak sizzles on the grill. A pot of wild rice simmers on the side. Add a freshly baked sourdough roll, a frosty glass of beer and a dish of hand-cranked ice cream, and I've got a instant reminder of the importance of grasses.

Take away everything that comes from grasses, and I'm left with an empty plate. Yes, corn is a grass. So is rice. And wheat. And the grains used to make beer. Don't forget the cane sugar that sweetens the ice cream -- it's a grass, too. Cattle, of course, eat corn and graze on grasses, so beef, milk and butter come from grasses, too.

It took an Oklahoma botanist named Ron Tyrl to open my eyes to our dependence on grasses. My visit to the North Dakota prairie cemented the lesson.

As an agrostologist, a botanist who specializes in the grasses, Tyrl touts his favorite organisms as enthusiastically as I do birds. During the years we worked together at Oklahoma State University, he encouraged me to watch where I stepped, and I coaxed him to scan the sky.

One of his favorite topics is the dependence of human culture on the grasses. Global production of cereal grains is in the neighborhood of 1.5 billion tons annually. We get approximately 65 percent of the calories and more than half of the protein of our diet from grasses. And of course livestock, the source of meat and milk, depend on grain, too.

We also rely on grasses for our lawns, erosion control and in less developed countries, thatch, fencing and baskets. Add bamboo, a tree-like woody grass, and we can add a variety of tools and construction materials to the list.

But Ron's passion for grasses is not limited to their practical values. In fact, his love and boundless enthusiasm for grasses is steeped in their beauty and grace. He closes his eyes and lets the images and names tell the story. Amber waves of grain undulating across the rolling prairie. Big and little bluestem. Indian grass. Buffalo grass.

Then he pulls you even closer with a close-up photograph of the flower. Yes, grasses have flowers. Seed heads (the "grain") originate from flowers. But not showy flowers with bright colorful petals like roses or marigolds.

The beauty of grass flowers is subtle. Only those who make the effort discover the delicate and colorful parts that enable grasses to reproduce. Others never notice. The feathery, pollen-producing stamens may be red, yellow or purple. In the glow of a setting sun, the colors of grasses can span the spectrum.

Grasses link us directly to the land; without them we would perish. They make reasonable the notion that the land itself is a organism -- all its parts are interconnected.

So next time you fire up the grill, thank God for grasses.

## Birding ~~Searchers 4-13-97~~ (5/91)

For birders, April through mid-June provides nonstop anticipation, discovery and excitement. New migrants return almost daily. In early May, when the warblers move through, handfuls of new species can arrive overnight.

Two years ago, on the third day of May, I cracked my bedroom window at dawn and heard a blue-wing warbler, a yellow warbler, a yellow-breasted chat, a prairie warbler, a red-eyed vireo, several indigo buntings, a house wren and two scarlet tanagers. The following morning six more species arrived. I picked up Kentucky warbler and ovenbird by ear and confirmed rose-breasted grosbeak, cerulean warbler, magnolia warbler and warbling vireo by sight.

Spring migration is to birders what deer season is to hunters and trout season is to anglers. It's a time to rise early, traipse through the woods and spy on one of nature's most spectacular events.

A hunter may wait a lifetime for a trophy buck. An angler might dream for years of a mountable trout, bass or musky. Birders long for a May morning that drops a flight of warblers on their favorite birding spot... a morning before the trees leaf out and obscure the feathered splotches of color that forage among the treetops... a morning that's bright, warm and filled with more bird songs than one can hope to identify. Such a day is a trophy day for birders.

Those two days in May last year were my trophy days. It didn't matter that none of the birds were "life birds" -- birds I had never seen before. What mattered was that for a few days they came to my woods -- all the way from the forests and fields of Latin America.

You see, it's not difficult to see lots of different birds over a span of years in a variety of places. That requires only time and persistence. But to see 14 newly arrived migrants within 250 yards of your back porch in less than 48 hours is like bowling a near- perfect game or pitching a one-hitter.

The drive to see new birds or more birds this year than last year comes from within. In that sense birding is a competitive sport. The big difference between birding and most sports is the absence of spectators -- witnesses. Even when birding with friends, individuals often wander off on their own. The confidence of each identification is based on the birder's knowledge, experience and skill with binoculars and field guide. Among birders, rules and regulations are self-imposed. The only "referee" is the birder's own conscience.

I've logged many miles and gotten cold, hot, sweaty, wet and muddy in pursuit of birds. One quest that stands out is my search for a chestnut-sided shrike-vireo, a rare resident of the mountains of central Mexico no larger than a bluebird.

In the early 1980s I led a series of birding tours to Mexico, and the shrike-vireo was always a target bird. On each trip several people in the group saw the shrike-vireo, but I was never in the right place at the right time. A half dozen trips went by, and I missed the bird each time. Several times I glimpsed it flying off in the canopy, but l didn't see it well enough to count.

Finally, one November morning as the group walked along a mountain trail at about 6,000 feet, I spotted a shrike-vireo perched on a branch about 25 feet ahead. It had a huge hairy caterpillar in its bill. For several minutes I watched as the bird slapped the caterpillar against the branch to remove its irritating hairs. My first chestnut-side shrike-vireo was certainly worth the wait.

Such tales may seem trivial to those who have never discovered the joy of wild birds. But we all have our obsessions. Some are work; some are play.

The tie that binds them all is that the challenge that engages us in the first place comes from within.

Somewhere to the north the broad-winged hawks awoke to a warm September dawn. They were restless. Instinct -- ancient genetic instructions -- called them south. By journey's end, they would be in South America where lizards and snakes abound during the winter months.

Meanwhile, I sat perched atop a 1,400 ft. mountain in central Pennsylvania with a group of dedicated hawkwatchers. By nine o'clock the morning sun had warmed the surrounding valley, and convection currents of warm air began to climb the mountain wall. As the warmed air rose, cooler air rushed in to replace it, only to also warm and rise. These "thermal" currents (thermals for short) provide the lift that the broad-wings need to continue their southward journey.

Why flap your wings for thousands of miles when you can ride a series of thermals that will transport you hundreds of miles each day? Birds, and most animals for that matter, often favor efficiency over speed or power.

"Bird!" someone shouted as a dot appears on the north horizon. Moments later, another identified it, "Broad-wing." A third person clicked a hand-held counter, and a fourth recorded the bird on a data sheet.

Slowly the broad-wings moved through -- singles, doubles and small groups of three and four. Three or more broad-wings rising on a thermal are called a "kettle." Today the kettles are small, none more than a half-dozen birds.

After three hours several hundred broad-wings and sharp-shinned hawks had passed by. That's certainly an impressive number of hawks in just a few hours. But imagine what it must have been like on a September day back in 1987 when the watchers at this spot counted more than 5,000 hawks, most of them broad-wings. Lots of sore necks and tired eyes to be sure.

Each year hawk-watchers count about 16,000 hawks at this spot. In 1987 the total soared to 30,120. More than 14,000 of those birds were broad-wings.

Where is this special place, you ask? I can't say. It's too small and dangerous a place for large numbers of people. There is very little parking, and the highway at the top of the mountain makes a hairpin turn at the crossing point to get to the observation area. Furthermore, the top of the mountain is strewn with giant, jagged rocks that require nimble feet in sturdy boots. I certainly wouldn't take my girls there.

But that doesn't mean you can't watch hawks. An even better hawkwatching spot (20,000 birds per year) is just a short drive away. Located on Kittatinny Ridge between Reading and Allentown, Pa., Hawk Mountain is the premier hawk-watching location in North America.

The hawkwatching season extends from August into December, but each species passes through at generally predictable times. September, for example, brings thousands of broad-wings and the peak of the osprey and kestrel flights. Sharp-shinned hawks, the ones that eat song birds at backyard bird feeders, dominate October counts. Red-tailed hawks, which can be seen throughout the fall, and golden eagles peak in November.

The "best" time to visit Hawk Mountain, or any hawkwatching spot, is difficult to predict. Weather plays a key role in determining success on any given day. A late September or early October day with the following conditions improve the chances of hitting a great day: shortly after the passage of a low pressure system, winds out of the north or west, falling temperatures and rising barometric pressure.

But even if you hit an off day at Hawk Mountain, you'll have a great time. Hiking trails criss-cross the 2,200-acre sanctuary and a magnificent Visitor's Center makes even a visit on a rainy day worth the trip.

## Yellowstone Wolves (12/94)

Back in 1909 Aldo Leopold, the man who would one day develop the science of wildlife management, was a young and inexperienced Forest Service crew leader in New Mexico. While eating lunch on a rimrock high above the Blue River, Leopold and his men noticed an animal crossing the turbulent river. At first, they thought it was a deer. Soon, however, they realized it was a wolf. Nearby a half-dozen grown pups played in the willows. In 1944 Leopold recalled the encounter in a short essay entitled, "Thinking Like A Mountain."

In those days, Leopold recalled, wolves were varmints, killers to be killed. Moments after recognizing the wolves, the entire crew was "pumping lead into the pack, but with more excitement than accuracy."

By the time Leopold and his crew clambered down the hillside, the old bitch lay quietly, "a fierce green fire dying in her eyes. I realized then, and have known ever since, that there was something new to me in those eyes -- something known only to her and to the mountain. I was young then and full of trigger-itch; I thought that because fewer wolves meant more deer, that no wolves would mean hunters' paradise. But after seeing the green fire die, I sensed that neither the wolf nor the mountain agreed with such a view."

By the time Leopold wrote "Thinking Like A Mountain," the campaign to eradicate the wolf had succeeded in many states. The habitat destruction that followed in the wake of exploding deer populations that even hunters couldn't control convinced Leopold that large predators were irreplaceable.

"I now suspect," Leopold wrote, "that just as a deer herd lives in mortal fear of its wolves, so does a mountain live in mortal fear of its deer. And perhaps with better cause, for while a buck pulled down by wolves can be replaced in two or three years, a range pulled down by too many deer may fail of replacement in as many decades."

Leopold's wisdom and "Thinking Like a Mountain," in particular, rushed over me as I perused a recent press release from the Department of the Interior. The final hurdles have been cleared for experimental populations of wolves to be reintroduced to Yellowstone National Park and central Idaho.

Wild wolves from Canada will be captured and transported to Yellowstone and Idaho. A pack of 15 wolves will be released at each place. The project's goal is a population of 100 wolves in each area -- 10 breeding pairs and their offspring -- by 2002.

Of course, not everyone thinks reintroducing wolves is a great idea; it has taken years for the plan to be approved. Ranchers, in particular, fear wolves will decimate their livestock. To allay such fears, the introduced animals are classified as "nonessential, experimental" populations. That means they can be trapped, removed and even killed if the reintroduction is too successful. Without this designation, the wolves (which are endangered in the lower 48 states) would be protected under the Endangered Species Act. By using the Act's experimental population provision, the concerns of all interested parties have been addressed.

Years ago my wife and I saw a lone wolf in Glacier National Park. It had, no doubt, wandered down from Canada. We watched it for about 10 seconds and then, in the blink of an eye, it vanished. It was one of those rare wild moments I'll never forget. Even now, if I close my eyes, I can see the image of that ghostly lobo. When I think of the Rockies, I envision that wolf.

The Endangered Species Act works. It saved the alligator, the brown pelican, the peregrine falcon and the bald eagle. Now it's the gray wolf's turn. I couldn't be more pleased. I'm already planning a trip to Yellowstone so my daughters can hear a wild chorus that's been silent too long. If Aldo Leopold were here (he died fighting a brush fire in 1948), I suspect he, too, would smile proudly.

## *Roger Tory Peterson, 1908-1996* (8/96)

In 1934, at the professionally tender age of 26, Roger Tory Peterson published *A Field Guide to Birds* for Houghton Mifflin. At the time the publisher seemed less than enthusiastic. According to the New York Times, Houghton Mifflin printed only 2,000 copies and asked Peterson to forego royalties on the first 1,000 books. Since then, Peterson's east and west editions of his bird guides have sold more than seven million copies. And the Peterson Field Guide Series, numbering at least 46 titles covering virtually every realm of natural history, revolutionized nature study for amateurs. In essence, Peterson invented the modern field guide.

Roger Tory Peterson died on July 28 at age 87. He will be remembered as one of the great conservationists of the 20th century. Aldo Leopold inspired us. Rachel Carson motivated us. But Peterson, thanks to his vivid artwork and his straightforward writing style, coaxed millions of nature watchers into the field to identify the creatures that inhabit the world around us. Though he did not write and illustrate all of the field guides in the series that bear his name, his editorial input was evident.

It is difficult to protect and conserve nameless creatures. Peterson's field guides put names on everything from birds, mammals and wildflowers to mushrooms, fish and reptiles. His field guides have done more to promote "biodiversity" than all the books, magazines and television shows ever produced for that purpose. Naming plants and animals is the first step in conservation. Roger Tory Peterson realized that long before anyone else and for that the conservation community must be forever grateful.

Peterson's first love was birds. He was born August 28, 1908 in Jamestown, N.Y. and joined the Junior Audubon Club at age 11. A teacher encouraged him to draw birds. His first subject was a blue jay.

I met Peterson at Chicago's Field Museum back in the early 1980s. We were both attending a professional meeting of ornithologists. The evening at the museum was a social gathering, not a formal event to meet Roger Tory Peterson. Yet everywhere he went, a line of admirers followed. I finally screwed up the courage to get in line. I listened as he greeted every fan as if each was an old friend. His voice was soft and sincere.

When it was my turn, I was most impressed by his hands. His grip was firm, but his touch was so soft -- the hands of an artist. Our conversation was brief, and as I recall, I asked only one question. Was it true, as I had read, that as a boy he fed birds hemp seeds? He winked and told me it was. We spoke for just a few minutes about birds, wildflowers and butterflies. Throughout the duration of the meeting, he nodded or said hello when our paths crossed. Surely he didn't remember me. I suspect he was routinely kind to even vaguely familiar faces.

My lasting impression is that Roger Tory Peterson was an unusual man, a gentle man and a gentleman.

Fortunately Peterson received many honors before he died. In 1984 the Roger Tory Peterson Institute of Natural History was formed in Jamestown, N.Y. to further his efforts in conservation education. His many national and international honors include the Presidential Medal of Freedom, the United

States' highest civilian honor, two nominations for the Nobel Peace Prize and 22 honorary doctorates from American universities.

Tributes usually emphasize how much a person will be missed. Roger Tory Peterson's legacy will live on forever. No artist, ornithologist, writer or conservationist has had a greater influence on America's environmental psyche. My library tells me so.

## Green Quotes

Several times I have commemorated Earth Day by printing quotations with environmental implications. These are some of my favorites.

*"To keep every cog and every wheel is the first precaution of intelligent tinkering."* Aldo Leopold

*"What is man without the beasts? If all the beasts were gone, men would die from a great loneliness of spirit. For whatever happens to the beasts soon happens to the man. All things are connected."* Chief Seattle

*"Only in the last moment of human history has the delusion arisen that people can flourish apart from the rest of the living world."* E. O. Wilson

*"We reached the old wolf in time to watch a fierce green fire dying in her eyes... I thought that because fewer wolves meant more deer, that no wolves would mean hunters' paradise. But after seeing the green fire die, I sensed that neither the wolf nor the mountain agreed with such a view."* Aldo Leopold

*"I now suspect that just as a deer herd lives in mortal fear of its wolves, so does a mountain live in mortal fear of its deer."* Aldo Leopold

*"The thing the ecologically illiterate don't realize about an ecosystem... is that it's a system.... A system has order, a flowing from point to point. If something dams that flow, order collapses. The untrained might miss that collapse until it was too late. That's why the highest function of ecology is understanding the consequences."* Frank Herbert

*"The 'control of nature' is a phrase conceived in arrogance, born of the Neanderthal age of biology and philosophy, when it was supposed that nature exists for the convenience of man."* Rachel Carson

*"Conservation is a state of harmony between land and man."* Aldo Leopold

*"There is a curiously persistent popular belief that if wild animals are left alone, they will flourish in wilderness areas and reach an 'optimum population' in balance with other species in the ecosystem; but this is not so."* Barry Lopez

*"The long fight to save wild beauty represents democracy at its best. It requires citizens to practice the hardest of virtues -- self-restraint."* Edwin Way Teale

*"Arresting global population growth should be second in importance only to avoiding nuclear war on humanity's agenda."* Paul and Anne Ehrlich

*"... from the beginning of humanity's appearance on earth to 1945, it took more than ten thousand generations to reach a world population of 2 billion people. Now, in the course of one human lifetime -- mine -- the world population will increase from 2 to more than 9 billion, and it is already more than halfway there."* Al Gore

*"We simply need that wild country available to us, even if we never do more than drive to its edge and look in. For it can be a means of reassuring ourselves of our sanity as creatures, a part of the geography of hope."* Wallace Stegner

*"There are two spiritual dangers in not owning a farm. One is the danger of supposing that breakfast comes from the grocery, and the other that heat comes from the furnace."*
Aldo Leopold

*"Nature is not easy to live with. It is hard to have rain on your cut hay, or floodwater over your cropland, or coyotes in your sheep; it is hard when nature does not respect your intentions, and she never does exactly respect them. Moreover, such problems belong to all of us, to the human lot. Humans who do not experience them are exempt only because they are paying (or underpaying) other humans such as farmers to deal with nature on their behalf."* Wendell Berry

*"The last word in ignorance is the man who asks of an animal or plant: 'What good is it?'"* Aldo Leopold

## Ten Years and Counting (6/96)

Each year I seem to get older faster. I suppose that's because as we age, each passing year represents a smaller fraction of our life. When I was 10, for example, a year was one-tenth of my life. Now a year represents just a bit more than two percent of my life. I think that's why adults, not children, use the phrase, "Time flies."

I'm particularly aware of time flight this summer because it marks the 10th anniversary of my first column. It appeared in the now defunct *Pittsburgh Press*, and the topic was hummingbirds. Since then I've written nearly 500 columns or approximately 300,000 words. Today this column appears, under various names, in more than 20 newspapers from Wisconsin, Michigan and Illinois to Pennsylvania, Ohio, West Virginia and Connecticut, and its circulation exceeds 1.2 million readers.

81

Though I cover everything from birds and bats to fungi, outdoor travel and wildflowers, my favorite part of writing a weekly column is the feedback I get from readers. I haven't kept a detailed log, but I'm sure I've received more than 8,000 pieces of mail these last 10 years. I cannot answer every letter, but I read them all. Many spark column ideas. And surprisingly, many ask how I ended up with a Ph.D. writing a nature column in West Virginia. Today, answering that question seems appropriate.

I grew up in rural Montgomery County, Pa. and was fascinated with animals for as long as I can remember. I recall seeing my first hummingbird in a neighbor's flower garden while delivering newspapers. I collected insects, turtles, frogs, salamanders and snakes and occasionally managed to catch a chipmunk. My parents tolerated my peculiar ways, but usually insisted I keep my finds for just a few days. They knew better than I that wild animals make poor pets.

My college years took me first to the University of Delaware for a degree in entomology (the study of insects), then to Northern Arizona University for a master's degree in biology and finally to Michigan State University for a Ph.D. in wildlife ecology. In Arizona I studied the feeding ecology of prairie dogs; in Michigan my research focused on the nesting ecology of farmland birds.

My career goal was to be a research biologist for a state or federal agency, but when I went job hunting in 1980, I landed in the zoology department at Oklahoma State University. After a few years, my wife and I realized we didn't want to spend the rest of our careers in Oklahoma watching roadrunners and coyotes. We longed for the verdant woods of the east.

So we took the biggest chance of our lives. We bought 95 acres of West Virginia heaven, I quit my job, and we moved east. That was in August 1985. We spent eight months making an abandoned farm house livable.

Meanwhile, we needed to make a living. Linda was an established freelance writer, so with her as my mentor, I decided to write a nature column for newspapers. I dove into the project oblivious to how difficult it is to break into the freelance newspaper world. Not knowing any better, I submitted a few samples to the *Pittsburgh Press*. A few weeks later, I hit the jackpot. An editor called to say he liked the idea and would use the column twice a month. Within a year, I added four more papers, and I had a weekly commitment. Adding new papers has come slowly, but I'm averaging two new papers per year.

In addition to my column, I write for magazines, I write books, I occasionally lead birding tours to Mexico, I lecture, and for four years I've hosted a weekly, nature-oriented radio talk show in Wheeling, W.Va. In short, I'm a lucky guy. I live in the woods, and I enjoy what I do. Thanks to you for helping me make my dreams come true.

## *'Twas the Morning of Christmas*    (12/88)
(with apologies to Clement C. Moore)

Twas the morning of Christmas,
And all 'round the house,
The feeders were empty,
Not enough for a mouse.

Each feeder was hung
From its perch with great care,
But on this frosty morning,
The cupboards were bare.

Tubes, trays and suet bags...
Too many to mention.
In the Christmas Eve rush
They'd escaped my attention.

The rising sun on the breast of the new fallen snow,
Accented the vacuum in the feeders below.
I couldn't believe it, I'd stayed up too late.
I'd forgotten my birds on this most special date.

A flock of birds waited in dawn's early light,
Reminding me clearly of last night's oversight.
Impatiently they perched in an old apple tree,
Hungry and anxious, some scolded me.

Ashamed and embarrassed, I flew down the stairs,
I whistled and shouted like a big angry bear.
"Now Linda, now Nora, and Emma, you too.
We've got empty feeders, there's so much to do!"

I spoke no more words, and we all went to work,
We filled every feeder, I'd been such a jerk.

The birds quickly forgave me and flocked to the food,
I knew in moment, they'd lost their foul mood.

Cardinals and titmice and nuthatches, too,
Were the first to arrive at my backyard bird zoo.

The black-oil seeds disappeared with great speed,
I smiled contently, I'd fixed my misdeed.

Then finches and siskins sought the feeder with thistle,
They flew so intently, each looked like a missile.

Soon sparrows and juncos ventured onto the tray,
Ravenously joining the late breakfast fray.

Even the water dish pulled in a crowd,
Those six thirsty chickadees were certainly loud.

When finally woodpeckers found the replenished suet,
We were completely forgiven, and the whole family knew it.

I began to feel better, I'd made up for my goof,
When suddenly a voice caught my ear from the roof.
(You may not believe this, but I swear it's the truth.)

From a perch at the top, sang a sassy Blue Jay,
"Happy Christmas to all, and to all a good day!"

# Part 3

# Adventure/Travel

## *Whalewatching*

BAR HARBOR, Maine -- "Get ready, folks! The captain just saw a finback surface about a mile straight ahead."

Zack Klyver seemed to enjoy showing whales to others as much as he enjoys seeing them himself. And as the on-board naturalist of the "Friendship IV", a whale-watching boat based in Bar Harbor, Klyver certainly gets to see plenty of whales. All summer long, several times a day the "Friendship IV" takes eager whale watchers 26 miles out to sea to get a glimpse of these great beasts.

In June my family bought tickets, and we crossed our fingers. I was skeptical. The brochure promised we'd see whales. If we didn't, every passenger would get a free ticket for another trip. But I thought we might glimpse a fin a half mile away. Never have I been so delightfully wrong.

Marc Brent, captain and owner of the brand new, $1.5 million high speed catamaran, raced ahead at full speed. At 30 miles per hour, it took just a minute to get close enough for a good look. As we approached, Brent slowed down so the boat wouldn't spook the whales. Soon we had a pod of four finbacks in an arc around the bow. Even a hundred yards away, we could tell they were huge. Second only to the blue whale as the planet's largest animal, the finbacks surfaced repeatedly.

As they arched above the surface of the ocean, a cloud of misty air exploded from their blow holes. Carbon dioxide out, oxygen in. It looked like a plume of smoke and was easy to spot even half a mile away.

Each finback surfaced four or five times, then dove deeply for another meal of small fish and invertebrates. In the course of a typical day a 70-ft. long, 60-ton finback might eat 6,000 pounds of food. But having just returned from a winter-long fast on their warm southern wintering grounds, their gluttony is understandable.

Unlike the more glamorous and picturesque humpback whales, whose songs can be heard on tapes and CDs and whose images grace myriad postcards and posters, finbacks surface and dive without exposing their tails. Only the center two-thirds of their body emerges as they come up for air.

We spent more than a hour with two groups -- a total of nine finbacks. Because each underwater feeding trip lasts just four to six minutes, we saw them surface repeatedly.

Just when we thought whale watching couldn't get any better, we got the thrill of our lives. Twice the giant finbacks surfaced within 25 yards of the boat -- one group on either side of the boat. I haven't heard so much "oo"-ing and "ah"-ing since Philadelphia's Bicentennial fireworks display. At one point, I had a bird's eye view of a blow hole -- it could have swallowed my leg.

If our whale watch affected my daughters as profoundly as it did my wife and me, Shalaways will be telling this whale of a tale for generations to come. The images of those great whales, almost close enough to touch, will linger forever. It's hard to explain, but those whales touched us. It's been two weeks since we saw them, but we're still talking about them. "Save the Whales" has become more than just a slogan. Certainly creatures so magnificent, so mammoth are worth protecting. If the planet has a soul, perhaps it lives in the great whales.

Whale watching cruises are popular all along the Atlantic coast, from Maryland to Maine, so if your vacation takes you to the coast this summer, plan a whale watching trip. And if you find yourself in Bar Harbor, find the "Friendship IV." Captain Marc Brent knows whales.

## Dakota Dreams                                        (7/92)

On the western edge of the Central Time Zone in late June, twilight lingered until about 10:30 p.m. We arrived at Sitting Bull's burial site (one of several, we later discovered) across the Missouri River from Mobridge, South Dakota at sunset. An evening chorus of western meadowlarks echoed all around us as my wife explained to Nora who Sitting Bull was -- the famous Sioux Indian chief who helped defeat Custer.

Nearby another marker honored Sakakawea (a.k.a. Sacagawea), the young Indian women who led Lewis and

Clark up the Missouri River, across the Rockies and down to the Pacific Ocean. Thanks largely to her knowledge of the people, their languages and the fact that she carried a small baby clearly indicating this was not a war party, Lewis and Clark trip completed their journey and lost only one man. He died of appendicitis.

Lewis and Clark, commissioned by President Thomas Jefferson to explore the northwest territory, were two of the most important naturalists in history. They described, catalogued and collected specimens all along the way. We were following their trail through North Dakota, where they spent more time than anywhere else.

Heading into North Dakota we followed the Lewis and Clark Trail northward along the Missouri River. Highways 1804 and 1806 parallel the trail. (Paving of the entire route has recently been competed.) Key historic sites along the way are marked.

Fort Abraham Lincoln, Fort Mandan and the Knife River Indian Villages National Historic Site commemorate the people and places Lewis and Clark encountered during their time in North Dakota.

Hours of driving along the Trail on paved road in a motorhome made it difficult to imagine how laborious, dangerous and adventurous the Lewis and Clark expedition must have been. Though I'd read their journals beforehand, only by retracing the trail and seeing the few remaining free-flowing stretches of the mighty Missouri River could I truly appreciate the journey.

From St. Louis to the source of the Missouri in the Rockies, the trip was all upstream in a keelboat manufactured in Pittsburgh.. Then overland across the Continental Divide to the source of the Columbia River and on to the Pacific Ocean. Then back again to St. Louis. More than 8,000 miles in two years, four months and nine days.

Three days on the Lewis and Clark Trail primed us for the rest of our tour of North Dakota. We spent two days at Cross Ranch State Park, which sits nestled among the cottonwoods on the banks of the Missouri River about 40 miles north of Bismarck. Within walking distance, the adjoining 6,000 acre Cross Ranch Nature Preserve, gives visitors a sense of prairie life. Rolling hills, a sea of grasses, colorful wildflowers, ceaseless winds, distant horizons, bobolinks singing on the wing, a herd of bison in the distance. Now we could imagine what life was once like from the Mississippi River to the foothills of the Rockies.

We headed west to Theodore Roosevelt National Park. The Sioux called the region, "Mako Shika," which means "land bad." And no wonder. The rugged canyons, ravines, bluffs and chasms of the Badlands no doubt posed great hardships for the nomadic Sioux. But today, Interstate 94 crosses the southern edge of the park, and long scenic drives meander through the park's South and North Units.

Late one day and early the next we toured the South Unit. A herd of bison along the Little Missouri River conjured up images of "Dances With Wolves." Only patient, unhurried visitors see much beyond the roadside prairie dog towns. Coyotes, elk, mule deer and pronghorn roam freely, but blend into the landscape. Overhead, golden eagles soar. And underfoot, rattlesnakes slither. We saw two.

From Teddy Roosevelt we headed north, then east and south, to visit a handful of North Dakota's many wildlife refuges. Far off the beaten track, these refuges were, to our delight, lonely places. Save for birds and deer, we had each refuge to ourselves.

On our last day in North Dakota we met a farmer named Monty Schaefer. He listened proudly as we raved about the prairie -- its cool breezes, endless sky and a colorful landscape that changes from hour to hour. He agreed, "It's hard to just see North Dakota. You must experience it."


## *Quiet Water Canoeing* (5/94)

The summer of 1993 was a wild one for Linda and me. We spent three months searching for wildlife on their terms on their turf. All our encounters occurred on water -- quiet water -- water without a current. In our case, it was the lakes of Pennsylvania. We traveled more than 5,000 miles by car and paddled hundreds more as we criss-crossed the state in search of the best quiet water for a new book, *Quiet Water Canoe*

*Guide: Pennsylvania* (1994, Appalachian Mountain Club Books). The book is a guide to both canoeing and wildlife watching at our 66 favorite lakes.

Paddling a canoe on a lake -- quiet water canoeing as opposed to running whitewater on rivers -- is one of the best ways to observe wildlife. We describe it as taking a "nature walk on water." Animals seem to fear people in a canoe less than when they are on foot.

Another big plus for quiet water canoeing is that anyone can do it. The only strength required is for getting the canoe on and off the car. It's a great way for parents, kids and grandparents to share an outdoor adventure. You might sneak up on a great blue heron, discover an osprey nest or hit the jackpot like we did one August morning at Sinnemahoning State Park's George B. Stevenson Reservoir in Cameron County.

We pulled into the parking lot at the boat launch and immediately saw a mature bald eagle perched across the narrow lake. Several minutes later, we discovered another individual in a nearby tree when it swooped from its lofty perch toward the water. The absence of a white head and tail identified it as a juvenile.

With images of eagles still fresh on our minds, we paddled north. Suddenly the water ahead rippled. A river otter! We watched it dive and surface three times. Nearby we found a mud slide -- the kind otters love to make.

Unfortunately, river otters often get a bad rap from fishermen. Though these overgrown members of the weasel family are indeed primarily piscivorous, crayfish, frogs, waterfowl and many other aquatic animals are also important foods. Furthermore, food habit studies of otters consistently report three interesting trends:

1) Otters do not specialize in particular species of fish.

2) They typically eat the species that are most abundant in any given area.

3) And they eat slow swimming fish more often than faster swimming fish. In other words, otters eat whatever happens to be easiest to catch. They eat many more suckers, carp, shiners, sunfish and catfish than they do trout, bass or pike.

No account of quiet water would be complete without a beaver tale. Our most memorable encounter occurred at dusk one warm summer evening on Hill's Creek Lake in Hill's Creek State Park, Tioga County.

We floated quietly among the lily pads on the darkening lake. Soon we began hearing the distinctive sound of incisors cutting succulent vegetation. Within a 50-foot radius of the canoe, four beavers crunched contently on water lily stems and pads.

Slowly I inched the canoe toward the nearest one. We got so close that even in the darkness we could make out its beady little eyes. Suddenly we were too close. The beaver slapped its tail on the water and dove under the canoe. It resurfaced not 20 feet away, slapped and dove again. And then a third time. What a show!

We sat among the lily pads, transfixed, as a full moon rose over the lake. Night sounds filled the air -- "banjo-plucking" green frogs, bellowing bullfrogs and in the distance the tremulous whistle of a screech-owl. Overhead, the wings of a small flight of wood ducks whistled as they passed through the moon glow. Finally, reluctantly, we added our own sounds -- the dip and drip of our paddles as we headed for shore.

## *Rafting West Virginia's New River*     (7/89)

It's not quite as fast as a speeding bullet, but it certainly is more powerful than a locomotive. The whitewater that dots sections of West Virginia's 1,000 ft. deep New River Gorge generates tremendous power and propels adventurous souls on a ride that rivals super roller coasters for thrills and excitement.

I met the New River on Whitewater Wednesday, an annual celebration of whitewater rafting. Visitors came from many eastern states, though most of the out-of-staters seemed to be from Pennsylvania and Ohio. Among the hundreds attending were lawyers, legislators, teachers, mechanics and businessmen. I teamed up with two state senators, a librarian, a radio reporter, a state bureaucrat and our guide, Marc Gabor of New River Scenic Whitewater.

On the bus trip to the "put-in" spot Pam Maples, one of the trip leaders, warned us to follow our guide's instructions. "If he says, 'Abandon ship!,' you abandon ship -- immediately. When he says, 'Paddle!' you paddle. This is not a cruise!" Maples emphasized.

By the time we put on our life jackets and helmets and boarded the raft, some of us wondered if we had gotten in over our heads. As it turned out, the warnings were just to prepare us for the remote possibility of disaster.

The trip exceeded my expectations. Because of heavy spring rains, the river was swollen and swift. We traveled 16 miles, dropping 240 feet along the way, in about four hours. And that included a leisurely 45 minute stop for lunch and several stops to swim.

The first few miles were curiously serene. Then suddenly -- Surprise! This aptly named Class III rapid got us wet and into the whitewater spirit. Soon after Surprise, we bobbed through Dudley's Dip (Class III), bounced through Double Z (Class V) and paddled madly through Miller's Folly (Class V). (Rapids are graded from Class I, a babbling brook, to Class VII, an impassable torrent.)

From his perch at the stern of the raft, Gabor steered and shouted commands. "Left side, forward! Right side, back! Now both sides forward!" The idea is that as long as you're paddling, you're less likely to fall overboard.

Our raft made the whole trip with no accidental dunkings. And even if someone had slipped out, Gabor had us well prepared. "Float feet forward, and keep your legs up. If you drag your feet, they might get wedged in the rocks and drag you under." Not surprisingly, everyone mastered this techniques at the first swimming stop.

Gabor also advised us not to swim to shore. "If you hit the eddy wall, it will pull you under," he warned.

Eddies are the reverse flows that follow the shores of rivers. The line where the downstream flow slides against the upstream eddy is the eddy line. Beneath it is the eddy wall, an irresistible hydraulic force that sucks trespassers under. It's one of the most dangerous parts of a river.

On the flats between the rapids, Gabor filled us in on the river's history. Ironically, the New is the second oldest river in the world. It supported people as far back as 15,000 years ago. The C&O Railroad completed a line through the gorge in

1873, and today the D.C.-Charleston Amtrak train runs the gorge daily.

In 1977 the New River Bridge opened and staked its claim as the world's largest steel arch bridge. Motorists could now cross the gorge in one minute, instead of the customary 40 up and down steep, windy, narrows roads. And in 1978 Congress designated 52 miles of the New River as the New River Gorge National River.

If you're looking for some cool summer excitement, try the New River wave train. It's fun, it's safe (if you do what you're told) and it's beautiful.

## *The New River's Gentle Side*      (8/93)

"Let's rock and roll!"

With that simple command, Dave Arnold, one of Class VI River Runners' four managing partners, signaled the start of our run on southern West Virginia's New River. But this was no ordinary whitewater rafting trip. The purpose was to acquaint a group of writers with the adventure and safety families with even small children can find on the Upper New River.

Arnold explained, "When outfitters started offering rafting trips on West Virginia's wildest river back in the '70s, local people thought they were crazy. But thanks to expert guides and the finest equipment, whitewater rafting evolved into one of West Virginia's growth businesses.

"Today's life jackets and self-bailing rafts make rafting safe even for small children," Arnold assured me. "Life jackets are required by all participants. They are designed to keep your head four inches above the water. And the self-bailing rafts eliminate the cumbersome chore of repeatedly stopping to empty a water-logged raft."

Any other questions I had about safety disappeared when I learned that Arnold guided Vice-President Dan Quayle and his family down the New River a few years ago. If Class VI is good enough for the Secret Service, it's good enough for me.

That's how my nine-year old daughter, Nora, and I happened to be on the New River last week. We joined five other writers and eight children for two days of family-style whitewater.

Each of our guides was an experienced professional who seemed to truly enjoy kids. First they laid down the laws: life jackets and helmets on at all times, absolutely no littering, and do what you're told. After the ground rules were firmly established, the fun began.

The first day we ran the fairly wide and gentle Upper New River. We had a choice of large, guide-powered rafts or inflatable kayaks called "duckies." Nora and I chose duckies. These little boats are extremely maneuverable, and even children can pick up the basic techniques in just a few minutes. Just in case anyone had a problem, there was always a guide in a kayak nearby. And if paddling grew tiresome, you just jumped into a raft. The smaller kids were in and out of rafts and duckies all day long. By the end of the first day, everyone felt confident and comfortable.

The second day on the river, we graduated to the Surprise Canyon section of the Upper New. Here the gorge narrows, and the gradient drops more quickly. The water is deeper, faster and more exciting. Screams filled the canyon each time we negotiated a set of rapids.

Toward the end of the afternoon our guides gathered us in an eddy just above a set of Class III rapids called "Surprise." They put all the smaller children in the rafts and described the duckie brigade's game plan. Surprise's surprise is a big swirling hole that likes to eat duckies and spit them out into a quiet pool below. If we stayed to the side, we'd miss the hole and get through easily. But if we wanted a thrill, we should paddle hard directly into the hole. If we had enough speed, we'd emerge wet, but still duckie-bound.

I opted to hit the hole. Unfortunately, I entered it sideways. The huge wave rolled me up the far wall and back into the hole. Seconds later (it seemed like an eternity), my life jacket popped me to the surface. I floated to the flat water below and waited for one of the guides to bring me my duck. Despite the unintended swim, my run through Surprise was the highlight of the trip (for both me and everyone who watched).

The New River Gorge also serves as one of nature's most spectacular outdoor classrooms. Kingfishers, herons and egrets fish the eddies, beds of water-stargrass flower beneath the swiftly flowing current and the river itself, the second oldest in the world, is a geological wonderland.

Those seeking bigger thrills (Class IV and V rapids) can try the lower New and the nearby Gauley River. And if you're an angler, the New River offers one of the finest smallmouth bass fisheries in the country.

Whether you seek thrills, exciting family recreation, overnight adventure or unparalleled fishing, the New River has it all. For more information, call Class VI River Runners at 1-800-CLASS VI.

## *An Alaskan Adventure* (8/91)

KODIAK ISLAND, Alaska -- Everyone keeps a wish list of places they'd like to someday visit. Alaska has always been high on mine. Last month I spent a week exploring Kodiak Island, home to spawning salmon, nesting bald eagles and the almost mythical Kodiak brown bear.

Clear blue skies and mild temperatures greeted me as I boarded a five-passenger Piper airplane. A 50-minute flight took me from the town of Kodiak to the native village of Akhiok on the southern tip of the island. From the air, a vast wilderness paradise revealed itself -- snow-capped, emerald-green mountains, hundreds of small turquoise lakes, cascading waterfalls and mountain streams.

In Akhiok I boarded a small boat and headed for the mouth of the Dog Salmon River. There, I was promised, I would catch fish. I've heard such promises -- wishful thinking might be a better term -- before.

But not that day. Not in Alaska. For three hours I waded the icy river and cast a variety of lures. And for three hours I caught fish. Dozens of them. Maybe 50 altogether. I stopped counting at 20. Most were pink salmon in the three to six pound range. A few were Dolly Varden trout. My casting arm and hand actually cramped and ached.

In the midst of the fish catching frenzy, I took a break to visit Paul Kuriscak , a technician with the Alaska Department of Fish and Game. He spends his summers in a cabin near the banks of the Dog Salmon enforcing fishing regulations and counting salmon as they move up the river to spawn.

He counts the fish at a weir, a structure which permits water to flow, but prevents the passage of fish. When he's ready to count, he opens a gate and uses a hand-held counter to tabulate salmon by the thousands.

Because the weir creates a bottleneck for the migrating fish, it's a favorite fishing spot for Kodiak bears. Kuriscak told me several had been visiting this spot every evening, so I might see some bears.

While we waited, he told me about the bears. Kodiak and grizzly bears are subspecies of brown bears (*Ursus arctos*). The key difference is size. Kodiak bears can stand 12 feet tall and weigh as much as 1,500 pounds. Most are smaller, but even eight-foot, 800-pound Kodiaks are big compared to mainland grizzlies, which may stand six or seven feet tall and weigh 300 to 700 pounds.

The reason Kodiak bears are so much bigger than mainland grizzlies is quite simple. They eat better. From June through September Kodiaks have access to a virtually unlimited food supply. Five species of salmon return to freshwater streams to spawn throughout the summer. They come by the millions, back to their birth streams to spawn the next generation and then die.

As Kuriscak regaled me with stories of bears he'd encountered, a lone sow broke through an alder thicket on the far side of the stream near the weir. She lumbered to midstream, grabbed a thrashing pink salmon, skinned it with two swipes of a massive paw and ate the fillets. She then tossed aside the rest of the carcass and grabbed another.

Over the course of the next two hours, three single sows, one boar and one sow with cub visited the weir for supper. Their appetites were impressive even for such large animals. I watched one sow eat more than 30 salmon before she wandered back to the seclusion of the alders.

I left the Dog Salmon understanding why Kodiak brown bears grow so big. They dine at an all-you-can-eat fish bar all summer long. And in the fall, after the salmon run, they gorge on the carcasses of the spent fish that litter the streams and rivers.

The next morning more typical Kodiak weather moved in -- fog, rain, wind. My guide this day, Ron Brockman, proprietor of Kodiak Nautical Discoveries, slowly maneuvered his 42-ft. "Sea Surgeon" (Brockman's a retired physician) out of the calm of a protected cove of Three Saint's Bay.

Suddenly a pod of five or six killer whales broke the surface of the bay. Brockman cut the engines and for 10 minutes we watched as huge dorsal fins repeatedly broke the surface. Occasionally one arched high enough to reveal some of the distinctive white markings characteristic of orcas. Then, as suddenly as they appeared, they were gone.

My dream trip was all I had hoped for and more. Australia and the Galapagos can wait. I'm already planning a return trip to Kodiak.

## *The Enchanted Islands* (1/95)

GALAPAGOS ISLANDS -- When I was a boy, I dreamed of a place where I could walk freely among wild animals. After more than 30 years, I found such a place -- the Galapagos Islands, located 600 miles west of Ecuador in the Pacific Ocean. Sea lions guard the beaches, giant tortoises graze in cow pastures and curious fish, sea turtles and even penguins investigate those who snorkel in the island's clear blue bays.

I spent the first week of January cruising the Galapagos with a group of 19 other curious naturalists. The tour had been organized by a friend of mine from Oklahoma State University.

My expectations were high -- I'd been reading everything I could find about the Galapagos for the last six months. I wasn't disappointed. To the wildlife on the Galapagos, man is just another animal, a benign part of the environment.

Our first stop was a sea lion beach near Wreck Bay on the island of San Cristobal. Though the afternoon was chilly, overcast and rainy, the sound of clicking shutters punctuated our first hours on the island.

That first night we cruised for about four hours and reached the island of Espanola by dawn. As we boarded the dinghy that would take us to shore, I felt a rush of excitement like my kids must have felt their first day at Disney World.

Within 30 seconds of leaving the dinghy, I was face to face with a four-foot long marine iguana. Its black skin blended in perfectly with the dark lava rocks that dominated the shoreline. On my knees for an intimate close-up, I marveled that I was one on one with the world's only seafaring lizard. In the background, much smaller lava lizards posed on rocky outcrops.

Though marine iguanas, like many of the plants and animals we saw, are endemic to the Galapagos (found there and no where else on earth), it was difficult to concentrate on them. At my feet red and blue Sally lightfoot crabs and Hood mockingbirds scavenged the beach for morsels of food. On a bush just 10 feet away, a handsome Galapagos dove watched us as intently as we watched it. Overhead, boobies and pelicans soared effortlessly between bullet-like plunges for unsuspecting fish. I was overwhelmed.

After about an hour, our guide led us to a colony of nesting blue-footed boobies. Boobies, boobies everywhere. Big boobies, baby boobies, even booby eggs. Related to pelicans and equally ungainly on land, blue-footed boobies are indeed identified by their bright blue webbed feet. We had to watch every step lest we trample eggs or chicks.

From there, we moved on to a colony of masked boobies. These stayed closer to the cliffs. Interspersed among them on the rocky ledges nested pairs of swallow-tailed gulls and red-billed tropicbirds. A waved albatross waddled toward the precipice, opened its wings and let the wind carry it gracefully skyward. Small ground finches and warbler finches seemed to follow us as we walked the well marked trail. And at several points along the trail, Galapagos hawks posed patiently atop small trees. It was all I expected and more!

For seven days the adventure continued. Each day brought new discoveries. On Floreana we watched green sea turtles copulate in the surf. On Santa Cruz we walked among the giant tortoises.  On Bartolome, I swam with Galapagos penguins, a peculiar sight on islands that straddle the equator. On North Seymour, the trail snaked through a frigatebird colony, where males inflated their scarlet balloon-like throat sacs and bellowed to attract and impress females.

In fairness, I must add that the trip was not without problems.  Most of us got sick for at least several days; two had to see a doctor.  One of the ship captains was a lecherous drunk.  One of our boats almost sank; its passengers abandoned ship one morning at 4 a.m. as their boat took on water and listed dangerously to one side.  And on some of our snorkeling outings, several members of the group were stung repeatedly by jellyfish.

The Galapagos are not for everyone, but my adventure is one I'll always remember and treasure -- warts and all.


## Mainely  Birds                                                (7/95)

HOG ISLAND, Maine -- Hog Island, a 333-acre National Audubon Society sanctuary, sits just a quarter mile off the Maine coast in Muscongus Bay.   At sunrise parula, black-throated green and Blackburnian warblers join Swainson's thrushes and winter wrens for the dawn chorus.  Throughout the day herring, great black-backed and laughing gulls patrol the narrows between the island and the mainland.  Offshore, double-crested cormorants and rafts of common eiders float lethargically between dives for food.  At night, the eerie sounds of saw-whet owls and common loons make memorable lullabies.

I spent the last two weeks of June on Hog Island.  I was one of seven instructors for two six-day ornithology classes. The classes are part of Audubon's educational outreach program.  Adults from all walks of life, 55 in each session, converged on the Maine coast to learn everything from birding basics to the intricacies of bird song and territoriality.

For me, each day held new discoveries.  Just a half mile from camp a pair of bald eagles tended its brood of two eaglets. Active osprey nests dotted many nearby islands. On a field trip to a sandy beach near Bath, we found two endangered species -- least terns and piping plovers. The sandy colored plovers proved difficult to spot. Only movement betrayed their cryptic coloration.

On an all-day boat trip to Eastern Egg Rock, about six miles from the mainland, we spotted the one bird most had hoped to see -- Atlantic puffins. The puffins nest here, and they did not disappoint us. As we circled the rocky seven-acre island, a half dozen puffins swam, dove, preened and flew. Overhead, endangered roseate terns crossed back and forth across the boat. The group's squeals of delight suggested a class of giddy children. Therein lies the joy of birding -- the thrill of discovery. A new bird brings out the kid in us. How often in our everyday lives do we see something truly new? Not too often. But when a birder sees a new bird for the first time there is a rush of excitement and satisfaction.

I had seen the puffins before, but one never tires of these black and white clowns with multi-colored bills. I turned my attention to those around me. I watched faces smile. I listened to the animated chatter. Watching others see a new bird was almost as exhilarating as seeing it myself.

During my stay on the Maine coast, I added four birds to my life list. On Eastern Egg Rock black guillemots outnumber puffins at least 10 to one. But they were new to me. Enroute to the Rock, Wilson's storm-petrels, small swallow-like seabirds, fluttered and hovered above the rolling waves, and a lone gannet rested on the high seas. And several times in several places, I saw groups of black scoters gathered offshore from rocky outcrops.

But a bird need not be a life bird (one seen for the first time) to be memorable. The Blackburnian warbler, orange throat ablaze in full sunlight, quickly jumped to the top of my list of favorite warblers. The elusive Swainson's thrush that finally jumped to a high exposed perch and sang for several minutes will always remain a highlight. And the loud, clear, seven-second long song of the winter wren still echoes in my brain.

I had never lived on an island, and, though my stay was brief, it confirmed the final lines of a poem by Rachel Field: "... Oh, you won't know why and you can't say how/ Such a change upon you came/ But once you have slept on an island/ You'll never be quite the same."

For information about next year's ornithology classes at Hog Island, contact National Audubon Society Ecology Camps, 613 Riversville Road, Greenwich, CT 06831.

## The Puffin Project (7/95)

EASTERN EGG ROCK, Maine. Too often our grasp exceeds our reach. We despair that one person cannot make a difference. So we muddle along.

Last month I met a man who is living proof that individuals can make a difference. In 1969 while teaching an ornithology class off the coast of Maine, Steve Kress discovered that Atlantic puffins and other seabirds no longer nested on many offshore Maine islands. They had been eradicated by fishermen before the turn of the century.

After long, hard winters subsisting on dried fish, fishermen flocked to the coastal islands for fresh eggs and meat. They would find seabird nests and smash all the eggs. They knew that within a few days the birds would renest and, if they returned, they could collect fresh eggs. They also killed adults for meat and feathers. By 1880, seabirds had been extirpated from many islands.

Eastern Egg Rock, a seven-acre, state-owned island sitting six miles offshore in Muscongus Bay, was the historic southern limit of puffins on the east coast. Coincidentally, it was also accessible to Kress. He wondered if he might be able to restore puffins to the island.

It took a few years to get the project started, but in 1973 he transplanted a half dozen two-week old puffin chicks from Great Island in Newfoundland (where they are still quite common) to artificial burrows on Eastern Egg Rock. Over the next eight years, Kress transplanted 774 more puffin chicks to Eastern Egg. The chicks were hand-fed fish for four weeks until they were ready to leave the nest. Puffins nest in burrows or rocky crevices, so they don't imprint on their nesting island until they leave the nest at six weeks of age. Kress explains, "We had to transplant the young puffins before they realized they were Canadians."

Now the waiting game began. Young puffins fledge at night when they are six weeks old. Alone, they head directly for the ocean. For the next several years they live at sea. Exactly where they go and what they do, no one knows.

An amazing 95 percent of the transplanted chicks fledged successfully. A puffin's first few years at sea, however, are perilous. Most were never seen again.

Concerned that any adult puffins that returned to the island would not come ashore, Kress placed hand-carved and painted puffin decoys on the Island to make it more appealing. The ruse worked. The first banded puffin returned to Eastern Egg on June 12, 1977. In 1981 Kress observed puffins taking fish to burrows; five pairs were nesting on the island. Last year 15 pairs of puffins called Eastern Egg Rock home; this year there are at least that many. Some are unbanded, which means adults are coming in from other colonies. Some of the banded birds are 18 years old and still breeding.

Today Kress helps reintroduce seabirds to islands all around the world, and he monitors nesting populations of puffins and other seabirds on five Maine islands. He works as a research biologist for the National Audubon Society and relies on a dedicated group of volunteers. They endure weeks, and sometimes months, on these islands studying seabirds during the nesting season. Living conditions are primitive and isolated.

Such work is not for everyone, but Jen Boyce, a three-year veteran from Vermont, says, "I love it! That's why I come back."

Individuals can make a difference. Steve Kress not only brought puffins back to Maine, he created a whole new science in the process -- seabird restoration. He has discovered, "It's not enough to just acquire islands; it takes people to actively protect seabirds."

If you have at least two weeks you could donate to the project, can live without family, friends and life's basic necessities and would like to study seabirds, contact Kress for more information at the Puffin Project, 159 Sapsucker Woods Road, Ithaca, NY 14850.

## Mainely Moose

Wherever you vacation this summer, chances are you will spend some time watching wildlife. Visit the shore and see great blue herons, gulls, terns and shorebirds. Head to the mountains for deer, squirrels and maybe a black bear. Or hit the western prairies and mountains for pronghorn, mule deer and bighorn sheep.

In any case, be careful. Don't get too close and risk disturbing the animals or injury to yourself.

In June, while visiting Maine, my family had a close call. It happened so fast, we were completely at the mercy of Lady Luck. Fortunately, she smiled that day.

We wanted to see moose and were told that other than along the highways marked with moose crossing signs, the best place to see these giant members of the deer family was Baxter State Park, which is about two hours north of Bangor. We stopped at park headquarters and asked where to go. We were told to hike to Sandy Stream Pond. The hike to the pond was less than a mile, perfect for a family with young children.

It only took us about 20 minutes to get to the pond and sure enough, we found nine moose. Actually, we heard them before we saw them, although we didn't realize it at the time. Four big bulls stood in shoulder-deep water. They were huge, many times the size of the lone white-tailed deer that drank from the far edge of the pond. Their massive palmate antlers enabled even four-year old Emma to identify them on sight.

Four cows were scattered elsewhere around the pond. One tended to a tawny-colored calf. The adults all foraged contently on aquatic vegetation they pulled from the pond's bottom. This pond-feeding not only provides these browsers with succulent food, it provides some relief from the North Woods' abundant mosquitoes and biting black flies.

The bulls were most impressive. Each time one plunged its head beneath the surface it completely disappeared for 15 to 30 seconds. Then it raised its head with a loud "Whoosh," and a stream of water cascaded down its large rack. This was the sound we had heard earlier, as we approached the pond.

So far so good. The moose put on a great show, and we watched, spellbound, from the safety of a shoreside trail. Before long, my ears detected some unfamiliar songs floating down from the spruce trees surrounding the lake. My attention shifted to Cape May and bay-breasted warblers. Meanwhile, Linda and the girls wandered farther along the trail. And as kids are wont to do, ours stayed in the lead.

Suddenly, with no warning, a large cow made a beeline to shore and emerged from the water between my wife and the girls. For a moment, Linda's heart stopped. Fifteen hundred pounds of moose stood between her and the kids. Every possible disastrous scenario raced though her mind. (With my attention fixed on dickie birds, I was oblivious to the entire drama.) The girls, on the other hand, stood quietly and watched in awe as the huge wild beast lumbered past almost close enough to touch.

Fortunately the moose was much less impressed with us than we were of her, and she disappeared into the woods as quickly as she had appeared. We closed ranks quickly and told the girls they had done the right thing by remaining quiet and motionless. And we counted our blessings that the cow had not felt threatened by the kids.

My point is that wildlife is wild, unpredictable and potentially dangerous. Don't feed wild animals. Don't approach them too closely. And don't harass them. You are on their turf, so treat them with the respect they deserve.

## *Laurel Caverns* (6/95)

UNIONTOWN, Pennsylvania. -- When I was a teenager, I did my share of stupid things. Most involved taking chances. Among the most foolish was exploring wild caves. Some friends and I went through a spelunking phase. We explored more than a few of the wild, unmarked caves that dot southeastern Pennsylvania. Inexperienced and untrained, we'd find hole in a field and, armed with just a few flashlights, disappear underground. And of course, we never told anyone where we would be.

In retrospect, I realize how dangerous wild caves can be. I'm amazed we never suffered a tragedy. We crawled through tight passages and forded underground streams.

Demonstrating that we still possessed at least an ounce of sense, though, we drew the line at swimming in a deep hole we once discovered.

Eventually I realized how dangerous amateur spelunking could be, so I concentrated on school and sports. I've never lost my fascination with caves, though, and in the intervening years, I've visited quite a few including Carlsbad Caverns in New Mexico. Guided tours in developed caves are safe and educational, but they lack the risk that appeals to kids.

Over the Memorial Day weekend I discovered the best of both worlds. I took my family to Laurel Caverns in southwestern Pennsylvania. I'd seen the billboards for years and finally decided to check it out. Laurel Caverns, a privately owned cave just east of Uniontown, advertises "family adventure." That means you can take a traditional guided tour or you can opt to explore an unlit, unmarked portion of the cave on your own. We chose the wild route.

After reading all the warnings and signing release forms, my wife began to doubt the wisdom of our decision. Maybe the kids would enjoy the guided tour more, she suggested. But Nora and Emma wouldn't hear of it. So after testing our flashlights and tightening our hardhats, we began the descent.

Laurel Caverns sits atop a mountain ridge and descends parallel to the slope of the mountain. Overhead lights illuminated the first few hundred feet. When we entered the "Dining Room," the cave went black. We had a map, so we knew the general direction we should go, but finding the small passageways sometimes proved a challenge.

The hole that led out of the Dining Room was narrow and dropped about five feet. We carefully worked our way through a series of passages and rooms. At times we crawled along on our hands and knees, and once we even had to slide a short way on our backs. At one point, we turned off our flashlights to experience total darkness. It was an eerie sensation.

The return trip, though completely uphill, seemed easier than the descent. The going was slower, though, because five-year old Emma needed help climbing some of the steeper passages. When we finally found our way back to the Dining Room, having been stymied only once by a dead end, we all felt a sense of accomplishment and relief. We were dirty, wet and tired and, despite a stable air temperature of 52 degrees Fahrenheit, we had worked up a good sweat.

If you're looking for a family adventure, consider exploring Laurel Caverns. My kids loved it. Nora, 11, thought it was one of our most exciting outings. In fact, she led the way by staying ahead and finding each new passageway. Although we spent almost three hours underground, we walked, climbed and crawled less than a mile.

And if you get lost? No problem. All visitors are carefully checked in and out of the cave. At the end of the day, if anyone is missing, cavern employees search until the missing are found.

Laurel Caverns is located five miles south of U.S. 40 just a few miles east of Uniontown and is open every day from 9 to 5. Just follow the signs.

## *Mill Grove* (1/92)

AUDUBON, Pennsylvania -- Mill Grove is more shrine than museum. Located high atop a hill overlooking the Perkiomen Creek in Montgomery County, Pa., the estate served as John James Audubon's home from 1804 to 1806. During this brief period in young Audubon's life, birds caught his fancy. Later he became the first wildlife artist to depict his subjects in natural settings.

Born in what is now Haiti in 1785, Audubon grew up in France and moved to America to supervise his father's estate at Mill Grove when he was just 18 years old. Captivated by Mill Grove's abundant wildlife, young Audubon spent his first years in America hunting, trapping, watching birds and sketching. He became a skilled outdoorsman, naturalist and artist.

While at Mill Grove, Audubon discovered that limp, lifeless models (he shot many of his subjects) made painting life-like images quite a challenge. "But alas! They were dead, to all intents and purposes, neither wing, leg nor tail could I place according to my wishes," he later wrote.

One morning Audubon awoke with an inspired solution to his problem, a solution that would characterize many of his future works. He dashed to nearby Norristown, bought some wire and, upon his return, shot the first bird he saw -- a kingfisher. He then skewered the bird's wings, legs and body until, "There stood before me the real kingfisher." This wire armature proved to be the tool that allowed Audubon to bring the victims of his gun back to life on canvas.

During Audubon's first year at Mill Grove, he made one of his greatest contributions to ornithology. He discovered a nest of phoebes in a rocky cave and attached "silver threads" to their legs. He hoped to see if the birds would ever return to Mill Grove. The next year, in the spring 1805, he observed an adult phoebe with a silver thread on its leg tending a nest. Modern bird banding traces its roots to John James Audubon, a silver thread and that phoebe.

These are just a few of the things I learned about Audubon when I visited Mill Grove over the holidays. Though I, too, grew up in Montgomery County, Mill Grove is one of those attractions many locals overlook. Like Philadelphia resident, nature lover and first-time visitor Michaele Walsh who vowed, "I'll definitely be back this spring!"

Since 1951 Montgomery County has maintained Mill Grove as a museum and wildlife sanctuary for all to enjoy. In 1989 it was designated a National Historic Landmark. It's definitely worth a visit.

The wall's of the house are decorated with many of Audubon's classic works, including a recently restored, life-sized original of a golden eagle taking a lamb. The other furnishing are early 1800s vintage, giving the house an historic appeal to even those with no interest in birds.

After touring the house, which takes about an hour, I walked some of the easy trails snaking through the 175-acre estate. Even on a gray late December morning I counted a dozen species of birds. A return visit in mid-May would no doubt be rewarded with a list of 30 to 50 species, including a variety of warblers and vireos.

On Sunday morning, April 17, I landed in Billings, Montana and began an 1,800-mile odyssey across Big Sky Country. For five days I birded my way across the nation's fourth largest state. By Thursday night I had seen 101 species of birds -- and most of the migrant song birds had not yet arrived.

The first stop was Makoshika State Park, just outside of Glendive in east-central Montana. We arrived at mid-day, so birding was slow. The main attraction at this scenic, little-known park is the scenery. As the sun set, the colorful badlands reminded me of the western Dakotas -- rugged, barren, beautiful. A brand new visitor's center explains the area's geology and clean camp sites are readily available. I'd love to have spent a few sunrises and sunsets there.

After dinner we motored farther north to Culbertson where we spent the night. At 4:30 Monday morning, we headed out for Medicine Lake National Wildlife Refuge. Refuge manager Tedd Gutzke greeted us and led us to a blind on a sharp-tailed grouse lek.

During the spring male sharp-tailed grouse assemble each morning on traditional mating grounds, called leks, where they dance, display and make sounds that might best be described as clucks and belches. Hen sharp-tails find these antics irresistible. (So did we.)

We sat cramped in a small blind and watched spellbound as more than 20 males fanned their tails and wings, stamped their feet madly and "sang" their love songs. Birds passed within 15 feet of the blind.

Females visit daily, sometimes for weeks, to check out the beefcake before selecting the "best" male. After mating, females go off on their own, build a nest, incubate the eggs and raise to the chicks.

By the time we arrived at the blind at dawn, the show had already begun. The birds flushed when we approached, but returned within 10 minutes.

Later, as Gutzke gave us a tour of the refuge, we saw thousands of ducks, Canada and snow geese, white pelicans, gulls and dozens of ring-necked pheasants. Though pheasants are now hard to find here in the east, Montana's healthy population attracts hunters from all over the country. Gutzke told us that last year pheasant hunters came to the refuge from 34 states.

On Tuesday morning we met Fritz Prellwitz, assistant manager of the Bowdoin National Wildlife Refuge. At the refuge headquarters a great horned-owl sat motionless in her nest in a tree just 25 yards from the building. A three-hour tour of the refuge once again yielded thousands of waterfowl and shorebirds including marbled godwits, avocets and black-necked stilts. We also saw several short-eared owls flying across the prairie just a few feet above the ground in search of voles. And a pair of coyotes played "cat and mouse" with a herd of pronghorn.

The next morning the alarm roused me at 4:30 for breakfast with Mike Schwitters, one of Montana's premier birders. He took us to a state wildlife area called Freezeout Lake and showed us virtually every duck that passes through the state, as well as five species of grebes -- western, Clark's, red-throated, eared and horned.

Among the day's other highlights were the dancing displays of several pairs of western grebes at Freezeout and a herd of more than 200 bighorn sheep on the slopes of the Eastern Front of the Rocky Mountains near Sun Valley Canyon.

Thursday, our final day, found us west of the Continental Divide exploring Ninepipes and Pablo National Wildlife Refuges and the National Bison Range. With Denver Holt, a Montana owl expert, we netted and banded a long-eared owl and inspected several nests. At the Bison Range we saw more bison, mule deer and elk than I could count. And at day's end, we visited a backyard in Missoula where Holt whistled in a western screech-owl.

Not bad for a spur-of-the-moment trip. Imagine what you might see if you took your time.

# *Colima*

Like many birds, I migrate south in the fall. When chilling winds, falling temperatures and early snowfalls foreshadow the winter to come, I pack my binoculars and spotting scope and head to Mexico.

December in Mexico is the dry season. But the images of blue skies and scorching sun I've come to expect were absent this time.

I just returned from 10 days in Colima, a tiny state on Mexico's west coast. It's a place I know well -- I've been there a dozen times in the last five years. But the first day, I knew we were in for unusual weather because it was so cool. After a morning of birding, I still hadn't worked up a sweat.

Midway through the trip, clouds moved in and the rains began. A drizzle at first. Then a steady rain. And finally downpours, accompanied by occasional gale force winds. Sounds like enough to ruin almost any trip.

But this was no ordinary trip. It was a birding tour. One of many I've led to Colima in recent years. Fortunately birders are a hardy sort. It takes more than foul weather to discourage them.

Unusually cool temperatures in the 70s made the first three days of the trip delightful. Our home base, the University of Oklahoma's Hacienda El Cobano, proved rich in bird life. In the hacienda's courtyard golden-cheeked woodpeckers, yellow-winged caciques, great kiskadees and social flycatchers greeted us. High in the canopy of a nearby royal poinciana rufous-backed robins and rose-throated becards foraged.

In the field just beyond the hacienda's outer wall painted buntings and black-capped vireos lurked in the underbrush. And in the distance inca doves called, "No hope. No hope. No hope."

In a nearby thorn forest white-throated magpie jays sailed by at tree top level. A family group of black-chested sparrows moved back and forth in the acacia thickets. And migrant blue-gray gnatcatchers and Nashville warblers seemed to be everywhere.

At 5,000 feet, in the shadow of the Volcan de Fuego, warblers stole the show. Crescent-chested, olive, hermit, black-throated gray, Townsend's and red-faced warblers flitted from tree to tree. Painted redstarts hovered overhead as they gleaned small insects from the surface of leaves.

A flock of 40 or 50 gray silky-flycatchers seemed to follow us along the mountain road. As we searched for it, a mountain trogon watched us from the safety of the darkened understory. And in the sky rough-winged, tree and violet-green swallows gave the group a 20 minute clinic in swallow identification.

On the coast, normally a hot and humid place, the cool dreary weather continued. It dampened our clothes and equipment, but not our enthusiasm.

San Blas jays flew from palm tree to palm tree. Flocks of groove-billed anis rested, wings extended, in roadside thickets. Crested caracaras and black-shoulder kites sailed by occasionally in search of the day's first meal.

Wading birds dotted the wetlands. Great egrets and roseate spoonbills stood quietly at the water's edge. Wood storks perched in the snags. Even yellow-crowned night herons stood exposed on the mudflats. A special treat for everyone was a reddish egret dancing awkwardly in its peculiar search for food.

Overhead, magnificent frigatebirds soared on the thermals, and brown pelicans rode the currents just above the surf's surface. Brown boobies patrolled the bay, folding their wings and plunging from the sky to catch fish that ventured too close to the surface.

Where the water's edge lapped the beach, shorebirds hunted for crustaceans, worms and other invertebrates. Long-billed curlews, wimbrels, willets and marbled godwits foraged undisturbed as we watched from a distance with 25x spotting scopes. Briefly a semipalmated sandpiper came into view. And on a far shore a flock of several hundred black skimmers rested quietly.

By trip's end we had tallied 212 species of birds. Not bad, given weather that would send many tropical vacationers home ahead of schedule.

## Mexico Revisited                    (12/89)

Tanned and tired, I just returned, from 23 days in Mexico. But I wasn't on vacation. My visits to Mexico are strictly business. I've been leading birding tours to the tiny west Mexican state of Colima since 1985.

The trips are sponsored by Elderhostel, an organization that provides travel and educational opportunities to anyone 60 years or older. Elderhostel's mission is to offer reasonably priced adventures all over the world on just about every topic imaginable.

This trip was particularly long because I had two nine-day, back-to-back tours separated by a few days of R&R. The weather was hot and humid, and biting insects were annoying, but the birding was great. Russet-crowned motmots, brown boobies and blue-hooded euphonias were just a few of the tropical species I encountered.

You may recall that about a year ago I wrote another column about a birding trip to Mexico. I described how I caught a hummingbird by hand. It was a cool morning in the mountains. The hummer was still lethargic, so I just plucked it off its perch. No such luck this time, but one night a few weeks ago I had a close encounter of another kind.

After dark one evening I led a group of particularly adventurous and ambitious birders through several sugar cane fields to a recently plowed hilltop. Once in place I instructed the group to shine their flashlights across the field. I explained that we were looking for eyeshine -- two reddish-orange dots that give away a resting pauraque. Pauraques are goatsuckers, not unlike our whip-poor-will, that inhabit much of Mexico. When not flying in search of flying insects, these nocturnal birds rest in the dark on open ground.

After just a few minutes, I spied some shining eyes about 75 yards into the field. We approached slowly and quietly until we were within about 20 feet. At this point everyone raised their binoculars and got a perfect view of the flashlight-illuminated bird.

The pauraque seemed mesmerized, so I told the group to keep their lights on the bird. I wanted to see how close I could get. Staying just on the edge of the beams, I was soon within five feet of the bird. Thinking I might be able to once again catch a bird bare-handed, I removed my cap, intending to use it

111

as a net, and advanced one more step. The bird was now just an arm's length away, so I made my move.

It wasn't even close! That bird was in the air before my cap reached my beltline. But it was still quite a show, and everyone enjoyed watching the stalk. In fact it turned out to be one of the highlights of the trip for those who participated.

If the pauraque stalk was one of the trip's highlights, I guess I should also share the low point. It came between trips. I became seriously, though briefly, ill. No, it wasn't the food or the water. (Staying well in Mexico is easy, if you're careful.)

I decided to hire a boat to give deep-sea fishing a try. I was in Manzanillo, the self-proclaimed sailfish capital of the world, for a few days. Sounded like a good idea at the time.

Needless to say, I didn't catch a thing. But even if I had, I probably wouldn't remember. I spent five hours sprawled on the bottom of the boat sick as a dog. Never again!

Fishing disaster notwithstanding, it was a great trip.


## *A Florida Fish Story* (10/94)

ISLAMORADA, Florida. "My favorite clients are beginners or at least anglers who have never been out on the flats," confessed fishing guide Richard Stanczyk.

Obviously, we were made for each other. Not only had I never been to the flats, I didn't even know what the "flats" were. But I was about to learn. From Bud 'n Mary's Fishing Marina, which Stanczyk owns on Islamorada in the Florida Keys, we sped south and east about 15 miles to a place where the ocean was only three feet deep. As the tide receded that September afternoon, the water level dropped to just 24 inches. This was "the flats."

Our quarry was bonefish, a sport fish made popular by George Bush during his White House years. Bush, like many anglers, values this modest-sized fish for its ability to fight like a tiger. Twice Bush visited Islamorada while president, and twice he went home disappointed. (The week before my visit, however, Bush returned and landed a 12-pounder.)

Stanczyk, who's been guiding fishermen for 17 years, is one of the local bonefishing experts. He spoke quietly as he stood atop an elevated platform on the boat's stern and poled the boat across the flats in search of "tailing" bonefish.

Bonefish are wary, so they must be stalked quietly, without a motor. In fact, bonefishing is best when the tide's moving, and the wind's blowing. With all that noise Stanczyk explained, "Hearing a poled boat is like hearing a pin drop in a hurricane."

As we searched the flats, I realized that bonefishing is as much hunting as fishing. You've got to see the fish before you can cast to them. When bonefish feed, they drive their snouts into the bottom in search of crabs and shrimp. Anglers scan the surface for their tails, which beat back and forth, driving the fish downward to the food. Hence the term "tailing."

Stanczyk then explained bonefishing strategy. "When we see tailing fish, I'll pole toward them. It's up to you to cast the bait either beyond the fish or in front of them. The idea is to drag the bait right in front of their noses."

My first cast landed just beyond a school of bonefish. As I reeled the bait across their path, a bonefish grabbed my bait and ran. The only person more surprised than me was Stanczyk. No one catches a bonefish on the first trip, much less on the first cast. I set the hook. The fish bent the rod -- and shook the hook.

I don't know why or how, but I stayed calm and continued a slow retrieve. The fish came back for more and struck again. This time I followed Stanczyk's instructions. I kept the bent rod high over my head. The fish took off, and the rod squealed as yard after yard of line disappeared into the sea. Whenever the fish eased up a bit, I reeled furiously. Then it ran off more line.

For about 12 minutes we went back and forth, but finally the novice angler prevailed. Stanczyk estimated its weight at about seven pounds -- modest by bonefish standards. But I was pleased, proud and on a roll. About an hour later, I caught another bonefish. This one weighed about six pounds. (We released both fish.)

The next day I boarded Scott Stanczyk's (Richard's brother) boat, the Catch-22, for a day of off-shore fishing. My good luck continued. I caught a barracuda, seven dolphins (the fish, not the mammal) and a black-finned tuna. The tuna and one of the dolphins fought for more than 15 minutes, leaving left my arms feeling like limp spaghetti.

The dolphins fought mightily and jumped repeatedly -- just like they do on TV. The highlight of this day was a dolphin that sailed over the side of the boat and landed in the container we used to hold our catches!

September and October are the "off season" in the Florida Keys. Rates are lower, people are fewer and the fishing is great. For more information, call 1-800-FLA-KEYS.

## *Dolly Sods* (10/90)

DOLLY SODS, West Virginia -- A piece of heaven crowns the Allegheny Plateau in West Virginia's Monongahela National Forest.

On autumn afternoons hawks and eagles ride the rising thermals as they work their way southward. To the east as many as seven mountain ridges dominate the horizon on a clear day. Beaver ponds reflect vivid images of blue skys, billowy clouds and fall colors. In water-saturated bogs more typical of areas far to the north, carnivorous sundew plants dot the nitrogen-poor soil.

Dolly Sods is more heaven than earth. But it has a dark side, too. In minutes a clear, sunny day can turn brutal. Rapid temperature drops, sudden fog, howling winds, unexpected rain and snow take unprepared visitors by surprise.

The Dolly Sods Wilderness and Scenic Area is a land of superlatives. Spectacular views, awesome topography, remnant biology.

Two hundred years ago a vast red spruce-hemlock forest covered the area. Early settlers cut hay from the many open bogs and marshes that dotted the area. They called it the

114

"sods" -- an Old English word meaning meadow or grassland. Dolly comes from the Hessian soldier, Johann Dahle, who lived there after the Revolutionary War.

The area remained pristine for about one hundred years. Then, in the 1880s, loggers cut the entire forest. They burned the slash to create pasture for livestock. Over the next 40 years Dolly Sods was completely destroyed. What we see today, though designated wilderness, is a far cry from its a colonial appearance.

But the scrubby second growth gives today's visitors more of a "top of the world" feeling. Whether hiking along the edge of the escarpment or driving the road that traverses the Plateau, visitors sense they can see the edge of the earth. The view puts the importance of individual humans into proper perspective. Each of us is as important as a single ragweed seed in an overgrazed pasture.

I traveled to Dolly Sods in early October to visit the Allegheny Front Migration Observatory (AFMO). Since 1958 volunteers have captured and banded more than 133,500 birds of 116 species in an area near the Red Creek Campground. More than 75 percent of the birds banded have been warblers.

The banding station sits on the edge of the Allegheny front at the top of a steep valley. Migrating song birds work their way westward up this valley to avoid the stiff, steady westerly winds that blow across the Front. When they get to the top, many fly into mist nets designed to capture birds. Volunteers quickly remove the birds and take them to the day's designated bander, who identifies, measures, bands and then releases the birds.

Thanks to long-term banding efforts such as these, ornithologists have a better understanding of the migratory habits of song birds. Though the station is open from mid-August until early October, different birds come through at different times. Cape May and
Blackburnian warblers, for example, peak during the first two weeks of September, while blue jays and kinglets peak in early October.

After spending a few hours at the AFMO, I realized that the volunteers weren't doing this just for its scientific value. Some of them spend weeks camped near the banding site so someone is always there to tend the nets. They do it because they love it.

Veteran netter Mel Hooker, a retired advertising agent from Ashland, Ohio, talks to his birds as he extricates them from the net. "Settle down," he coos. "It's not as bad as it seems. I'll have you out in a minute."

Bander Trudy Smith, a volunteer from Groton, Connecticut, adopts a similar approach. "C'mon, little fella. We need to know how old you are," she tells a struggling red-eyed vireo.

The AFMO welcomes visitors. If you get to Dolly Sods at the right time, be sure to stop by.

Or if it's just solitude, wilderness and maybe just glimpse of heaven you're after, visit Dolly Sods and plan to spend a few days. (Winter can dump 150 inches of snow on the area, so make it a spring, summer or fall trip.)

For more information about Dolly Sods, write to the Forest Supervisor, Monongahela National Forest, Sycamore Street, Elkins, WV 26241.

## *Mendon Ponds* (3/94)

MENDON PONDS, New York -- This sounded too easy. We were to go to the beginning of the nature trail and, as soon as we saw or heard black-capped chickadees, stop and hold out a handful of sunflower seeds. Harold Jauch, a friend from western New York, had brought me to this special place.

We had walked less than 50 feet when the flock arrived. We each held out a handful of goodies and in less than 30 seconds a chickadee landed on the tip of Harold's ring finger. It boldly looked him in the eye, then snatched a sunflower seed and took off. Seconds later another chickadee landed on his hand. The parade had begun, but already I was beginning to feel left out.

I needn't have worried. These chickadees dole out their magic equally. Within three minutes each of us had chickadees coming to our hands every 15 seconds. Over the next half-hour more than 100 birds came to my hand.

After about 20 minutes my arm grew tired, so I tried a new position. I turned my hand over, fingernails up, and spread a mixture of sunflower seeds, sunflower kernels, chopped peanuts and almonds across the tops of my fingers. I wanted to see just how close I could lure them. Along the way, I'd see which foods they chose.

After each visit I lifted my hand an inch or two. Soon I was holding my right hand about three inches in front of my nose and still the birds came. They were now so close I could barely focus my eyes on them. I could see the fine detail in each contour feather that shapes the body. We stood literally eye to eye.

When offered the menu of foods I now held, they clearly preferred the nut meats and sunflower kernels. In this very brief and unscientific test, I couldn't determine which was their favorite, though it was clear they shunned the sunflower seeds in the shell when kernels and nutmeats were available. Smart choice -- why bother shelling seeds when it's not necessary.

We had also been told that red-breasted nuthatches sometime come for handouts. This would have been a real treat because I see these northern birds only rarely at my feeders. I hoped they would come, but I didn't want to be greedy. Oh me of little faith. Halfway through our visit, a pair arrived. They seemed a bit more wary than the chickadees, but eventually they came to my hand at least eight times. In hand they are handsome, elegant birds. I quickly realized that this day was one I would never forget.

Though I see chickadees every day and have often trapped and banded them, having them choose to come to my hand was truly a thrill. They trusted me, just like they trust any other person who walks the trail with a handful of seeds. I wished my daughters could have been with me. I know how I beamed each time a bird came to my hand and can only imagine how their faces would light up. I'll bring them to this special place next year, I promised myself.

The best part of this story is that anyone can visit Mendon Ponds County Park. It is located on Route 65 about 10 miles south of Rochester , New York. More than 20 years ago a park naturalist patiently trained the chickadees and nuthatches to come to his hand. Over the years subsequent naturalists have maintained the tradition.

If ever you find yourself in Rochester between October and April, take two hours and visit Mendon Ponds. And don't forget, lunch is on you.

# Part 4

# Backyard Wildlife

# *Feeding Wild Birds*  (5/91, 12/91)

Occasionally I encounter people who argue that feeding birds is harmful. It ruins birds' natural foraging instincts, they say. Or, they contend, supplemental feeding disrupts birds' natural migratory patterns.

Nonsense!

Birds that use feeders either live here all year (permanent residents such as chickadees, titmice and cardinals) or spend their winters here to escape harsher conditions farther north (winter residents such as juncos, tree sparrows and white-throated sparrows).

Applying human logic to animal behavior often results in incorrect conclusions. Perhaps the naysayers have heard reports of declining populations of neotropical birds such as warblers and tanagers and assumed that winter feeding tempts migrants to stay north and die of exposure. Such a leap in logic may seem reasonable, but it's dead wrong.

Migratory birds head south when their biological clocks detect autumn days growing shorter. Regardless of food supply, when photoperiod reaches a certain critical length, migrants hit the airways. Eons of evolutionary wanderlust compel each new generation to make the annual journey. Besides, most migrants eat insects and/or fruits, not seeds.

Despite what you may read or hear elsewhere, it's OK to feed wild birds. And at certain times, feeder food can mean the difference between life and death. During cold snaps when daytime highs remain in single digits or during winter storms, some birds may be unable to find enough natural foods to meet their metabolic needs. Only if they have a dependable food source that requires little travel and search time can they survive.

Field work by two University of Wisconsin ornithologists supports this argument. Margaret Clark Brittingham (now at Penn State) and Stanley Temple studied banded populations of black-capped chickadees for three years. They compared the winter survival of birds that had access to feeders filled with sunflower seeds to those that depended solely on natural foods. Among their findings:

• Most chickadees that used feeders got less than 25 percent of their food from feeders. Sunflower seeds simply supplemented their natural diet.

• Nearly twice as many chickadees with access to feeders survived the winter compared to those birds that depended solely on natural foods. This differential survival was most dramatic during months when temperatures dropped below zero on more than five days.

On these frigid days, birds that had to hunt for natural foods spent most of the day perching motionless with feathers fluffed. Perhaps the time and effort needed to find food under these conditions uses more energy than the birds are able to consume, so they're better off conserving precious fat reserves by doing nothing. If the cold weather persists for more than a day or two, they die. Feeder birds, on the other hand, continued to use their dependable food supply.

• Feeder birds suddenly deprived of their food source switched easily back to natural foods and survived as well as those birds that never used feeders. That means chickadees do not depend on feeders.

So don't worry about taking a winter vacation. Your birds won't starve. They'll switch to natural foods or find another feeder. When you return, fill your feeders and give the birds a few days. They'll return.

If you've ever worried that feeding winter birds may do more harm than good, relax. Birds don't rely on our generosity to survive, except during those infrequent periods of extreme cold. Although they gladly accept the handouts, birds can usually survive without them.

Now, how about feeding birds during the spring and summer? Is this OK?

While it may seem reasonable to assume that natural foods become abundant as temperatures warm, it's not necessarily true. March and April can be the most stressful months of the year. Fall and winter foods supplies are almost exhausted, and new spring foods are not yet available. Most insects are still dormant, and plants are just beginning to awaken. So a dependable supply of supplemental food can be even more important in early spring than in January or February.

Furthermore, the energetic demands of molt, territorial defence and nesting compound the impact of declining natural food supplies. Though it's most obvious on male goldfinches in the April, many birds replace their feathers in the spring. Male cardinals, titmice, song sparrows, blue jays and chickadees already spend much of their days in song advertising their territories and vying for mates. And nest building begins in the spring, too. All these activities require energy -- food. Until new crops of plant and insects foods are available, supplemental foods are at a premium.

It's best to keep a few feeders full at least until trees leaf out in mid May. Progressively fewer birds use feeders as spring proceeds. Birds migrate or space themselves out to nest, but a few cardinals, mourning doves, chickadees, titmice, blue jays, woodpeckers, goldfinches and house finches visit feeders as long as food is available.

Keep one or two feeders filled all summer long, and you'll be amazed at the birds that continue to visit. Add a nectar feeder, a nest box and a bath to your backyard sanctuary, and you'll draw hummingbirds, orioles and wrens.

Perhaps the best way to make spring and summer feeding stations irresistible is to add live food to the menu. Most birds switch to insects as the weather warms; that's one reason we see fewer birds at feeders in the spring and summer. Take advantage of this shift in diet by offering a handful of mealworms or grubs every day. Live food attracts feeder regulars such as woodpeckers, chickadees, titmice and nuthatches, as well as migrant house wrens, catbirds, warblers, vireos, tanagers and orioles. Even bluebirds and robins can be lured to a feeding tray stocked with live food.

The big pay-off from a spring/summer feeding program comes when parent birds introduce their offspring to the feeders. The satisfaction and enjoyment that comes from knowing you've had a hand in the success of a brood of cardinals, chickadees or downy woodpeckers is hard to beat.

Feeding birds is an ideal family hobby and great way to introduce children to conservation, nature and the outdoors. And if you understand birds' needs, you can enjoy feeding birds all year long.

## *Selective Feeding: Who Eats What?*     (10/91)

If you feed wild birds in your backyard, you're in good company.  More than 65 million Americans feed wild birds and according to the U.S Fish and Wildlife Service, we spend more than $2 billion each year on bird food.  The obvious question is, "What's the best food for wild birds?"

The best way to attract a greater variety of birds to your feeding station is to expand the menu.  Rather than just filling an ordinary  hopper feeder with a generic bird food mix, think selectively.  By offering specific birds and groups of birds their favorite foods, you can lure an amazing variety of birds to specific areas of the backyard.

As we gain experience feeding birds, certain species become our favorites.  Many love cardinals.  Others prefer colorful finches.  Still others favor chickadees, woodpeckers or juncos.  So we set out to create or purchase foods that attract these particular birds.

The key to feeding birds is understanding who eats what. Most birds have specific preferences that, once understood, can be used to attract specific birds to specific feeders.  The "selective feeding" approach is perfect for anyone ready to step beyond a single all-purpose mix.

The table that follows lists common bird foods and the species they attract.  It is based on my own food preference tests and the best advice I've gleaned from many other references.  Refer to it whenever you wonder who eats what.

| FOOD | WHO EATS IT |
|---|---|
| Black-oil sunflower seeds | all seed-eaters, including woodpeckers |
| Striped sunflower seeds | cardinals, grosbeaks, blue jays, chickadees, titmice, nuthatches |
| Hulled sunflower seeds (no waste, no shells) | all seed-eaters |
| Niger (a.k.a. thistle) | finches, doves |

| FOOD | WHO EATS IT |
|---|---|
| Unsalted peanuts in the shell | titmice, blue jays |
| Peanut kernels (no waste, no shells) | same as above plus woodpeckers, juncos nuthatches, chickadees, crows, goldfinches, kinglets |
| Peanut hearts | starlings -- a poor choice |
| Nut meats (almonds, walnuts, pecans; no waste, no shells) | woodpeckers, blue jays, chickadees, titmice, nuthatches |
| White, red, golden millets | native sparrows,* doves, juncos, finches, cardinals, towhees, |
| Safflower seeds | cardinals, titmice, house finches, doves |
| Canary seed | doves, native sparrows,* finches |
| Melon seeds (melons, squash, pumpkin) | chickadees, titmice, nuthatches, blue jays, finches |
| Whole corn | turkeys, doves, blue jays, red-bellied woodpeckers *grackles, crows* |
| Cracked corn (not recommended for city or town use) | native sparrows,* turkeys, cardinals pheasants, doves, ducks, juncos, *house sparrows, pigeons, cowbirds, starlings* |

| FOOD | WHO EATS IT |
|------|-------------|
| Milo (sorghum)<br>Wheat<br>Oats | ducks, pheasants, turkeys -- poor choices for backyard feeders |
| Peanut butter | woodpeckers, chickadees, titmice, brown creepers, kinglets, robins, Carolina wrens, yellow-rumped warblers |
| Suet | woodpeckers, titmice, chickadees, nuthatches, brown creepers, kinglets, Carolina wrens, warblers, *starlings* |
| Orange halves | woodpeckers, yellow-rumped warblers, orioles |
| Currants<br>Raisins<br>Grapes | robins, bluebirds, mockingbirds, catbirds, Carolina wren |
| Mealworms | bluebirds, robins, mockingbirds, woodpeckers, chickadees, titmice, nuthatches, Carolina wrens, warblers |
| Water | all species, all year |

*Italicized* species are considered undesirable by most experienced feeders.

* Native sparrows include song, field, chipping, fox, tree, white-throated and white-crowned sparrows.

## Suet Recipe

### The Best No-Melt, All-Season Peanut Butter/Suet Recipe You'll Ever Make

One cup crunchy peanut butter
2 cups "quick cook" oats
2 cups cornmeal
1 cup lard (no substitutes here)
one cup white flour
1/3 cup sugar

Melt lard and peanut butter in microwave, then stir in remaining ingredients.  Pour into square freezer containers about 1-1/2 inches thick.   Store in freezer.

(Courtesy of Martha Sargent of Trussville, Alabama.)

## Woodpecker Trees                                    (2/94)

During a recent visit to the A.B. Brooks Nature Center in Wheeling, W.Va., I saw something I had never seen before. A pileated woodpecker repeatedly came to a suet feeder. Pileateds are the magnificent, crow-sized woodpeckers that live in mature forests.

I had first heard about this last year.  The naturalists at the nature center had told me they had three pileateds regularly visiting their "woodpecker tree."   But the birds never cooperated whenever I stopped by.  Last week I got lucky.

I was at the nature center taping a segment for a television show when the large crested woodpecker swooped into view and onto the "woodpecker tree."  The woodpecker tree is a special suet feeder designed especially for woodpeckers, though other suet lovers use it, too.  It consists of a 4x4 post anchored in the ground.  On the top half of the post, a series of inch-deep holes about two inches in diameter run down two sides of the post. The holes are about 12 inches apart. Only the two sides of the post visible from the nature center's viewing window are used; this prevents birds from hiding on the back side of the post.

Building a woodpecker tree is easy. Sinking it in the ground in the middle of winter is not. So I devised a simple variation. I cut a 2x4 down to six feet in length and used an inch-and-a-half wood bit to drill four 3/4-inch deep holes on the top half of the 2x4. I placed the holes about a foot apart. I also drilled two pairs of 1/8-inch holes through the 2x4 -- one pair near the top, the other near the middle. Next I cut two lengths of plastic coated electrical wire and laced them through the 1/8-inch holes.

Then I took my modified woodpecker tree out to a tree I can see from my office window and strapped it to the trunk with the electrical wire. The final step was filling the holes with suet and/or peanut butter. Soft recipes can simply be smeared into the holes. Harder suet blocks must be pressed or even hammered into the holes.

Once the woodpecker tree was filled and in place, I sat back and watched. Within three hours, nuthatches, chickadees and downy woodpeckers discovered the new feeder. It quickly became one of the busiest spots in the yard. Not bad for a feeder that cost less than five dollars for materials and took less than 15 minutes to make. When I get my first pileated, success will be complete.

Speaking of woodpeckers, I often hear complaints recently about woodpeckers drilling holes in wood siding. Everyone asks why woodpeckers do this and how to stop it.

Usually woodpeckers hammer on siding because of the sound it makes when it's tapped. It sounds like a hollow tree. Woodpeckers "drum" on hollow trees and other resonant objects such as metal chimneys, flashing and siding.

Drumming is one of the ways woodpeckers communicate. Each species has a distinctive Morse code-like pattern that only woodpeckers of the same species understand. When a woodpecker finds a particularly resonant area on the siding, it uses that area until a hole forms. In most cases they are not searching for food, so woodpeckers drumming on siding are not a sign that the wood is infested with termites or wood borers.

One way to handle the problem is to scare the birds away. This is usually a temporary solution, but it's worth a try. Place an inflatable owl or snake near the problem spot and the birds will avoid the area, at least for a while. By moving the "predators" to different locations every day, you may be able to keep the woodpeckers at bay until they discover a better drumming site.

Another option is to exclude the woodpeckers by hanging garden netting over the siding. This costly and unsightly, but it works.

## Hand-Feeding Wild Birds (1/96)

Last winter I wrote of a place just south of Rochester, New York where wild birds come to outstretched hands filled with food. The photos and letters I've received from readers who have since visited Mendon Ponds County Park reinforced my belief that having a wild bird come to your hand can be a near religious experience. Hand-feeding wild birds personalizes the connection between man and nature.

Fortunately, we need not travel to Rochester to hand feed birds. You can do it in your own backyard. For example, a reader from Pittsburgh, Anna Mae Martin, reported how she and her sister gradually gained the trust of a blue jay.

"In the summer of 1990 we threw nuts to blue jays that perched in a nearby tree. They would fly down, pick up the nuts, then fly back up to the pine tree to eat them. Sometimes they would hide them in the tree.

"One afternoon I was sitting on the back porch reading a book when a jay landed on the railing just two feet from me. I happened to have a few nuts in my pocket, so I slowly offered one in my outstretched hand. The jay grabbed it and flew off.

"This quickly became a habit. Any time I sat on the porch a blue jay (I assume it was the same one) flew down and took a nut from my hand -- and from my sister's hand, too. This continued for four years, until May 1993. It was such a joy to befriend a wild bird."

126

Training wild birds to come to your hand is not as difficult as it might seem -- if you have patience and time. Mid-winter is the perfect time to try it.

You've probably noticed how birds wait near feeders on cold mornings for a fresh supply of seed. Sometimes they come within arm's reach of me as I fill my feeders.

To get a bird on your hand, take advantage of both their boldness and hunger. Instead of filling the feeders on a cold still morning, stand near the feeders and hold out a hand filled with sunflower seeds or shelled peanuts. If you remain motionless, and if you can bear the cold, you might have a taker within 20 or 30 minutes. Often, however, it takes several attempts before a bird comes to your hand. And sometimes it doesn't work at all. But if it does, you'll remember the day forever.

Now I admit that standing motionless on a frosty morning is asking a lot. So here's another strategy. Build a life sized dummy, a scarecrow, and dress it in clothes you normally wear when filling your feeders. Put gloves on the hands and a hat on the head. Then place some sunflower seeds on the outstretched gloves and on the hat. Give the birds about 30 minutes to explore the dummy before filling the feeders as usual. Continue this until the birds start treating the dummy as just another feeder. This may take a week or two.

Then dress yourself in the scarecrow's clothes, gloves and hat, and take its place. Assuming you keep perfectly still, you may have birds on your gloved hand within 10 minutes. And if you put some seed on the hat, you'll have them there, too. (Be sure to have someone nearby with a camera.) After a few days, remove the gloves and you'll finally experience the featherweight bulk of a live wild bird. Chickadees, for example, weigh about as much as two nickels.

The birds most likely to come to your hand are chickadees, titmice and nuthatches, but the list of hand-fed birds is a long one. Remember, the key to hand-feeding wild birds is patience. And the rewards are indelible memories of silky feathers on outstretched fingers.

# Hummingbird Q & A

Hummingbirds rank as one of America's favorite summer birds. Their tiny size, brilliant colors, acrobatic flying ability and eagerness to use artificial feeders endear them to young and old alike. Because hummingbirds are so popular, they generate a never-ending supply of questions from their admirers. Here are some of the most frequently asked questions I have received over the years.

**Q.   How many kinds of hummingbirds live in this part of the country?**
**A.**   Only the ruby-throated hummingbird occurs and nests regularly east of the Mississippi River. The female lacks the male's bright red throat, so some people think two species visit their feeders.

**Q.   What's the recipe for nectar?**
**A.**   Add one part table sugar to four parts boiling water. Stir, cool at room temperature and store in the refrigerator. Dying the nectar red is not necessary. The red on your feeder will attract the hummers attention. And **never use honey** as a sweetener. Honey promotes a fungal disease that can kill hummers.

**Q.   How can hummingbirds survive if they just eat sugar water?**
**A.**   If they ate just sugar water, they would not survive. Sugar is nutritionally empty, but it contains lots of calories. Hummers drink nectar for the calories -- the energy. They obtain nutrition by eating soft-bodied invertebrates such as spiders, flies, aphids and gnats. Nectar probably makes up less than half their total diet.

**Q.   What kind of feeder should I use?**
**A.**   Spend 10 to 20 dollars, and buy a good hard plastic feeder. It should have perches so the hummers aren't forced to hover while they drink. Hummers legs are small, but they can and do rest by perching.

Be sure the feeder has an opening large enough to insert a bottle brush for weekly scrubbing. Hummers avoid moldy feeders, so keep yours clean. Rinse the feeder and change the nectar every three days. Wash it with hot soapy water once a week.

Glass feeders are usually difficult to clean, and they shatter when dropped. Soft plastic feeders leak because they expand and crack when daytime temperatures reach 80 or 90 degrees.

My favorite nectar feeders are the HummZinger, the HummZinger Excel and the Nectar Bar, all made by *Aspects, Inc.*

### Q. Is there anything else I can do to attract hummingbirds?

**A.** Landscape your yard with plants that have nectar producing flowers. Visit a local nursery or scan a gardening catalog and look for trumpet honeysuckle, trumpet creeper, coralberry, jewelweed, bee balm, various mints, rose of Sharon and flowering quince. All are hummingbird favorites.

A less conventional way of providing food is to put out some overripe fruit. Hummers have a field day feasting on the fruit flies. It takes a little extra effort to attract hummingbirds. But you'll find the rewards well worth the effort.

### Q. How can I keep bees and yellow jackets away from my hummingbird feeders?

**A.** Some feeders come with "bee guards," but I've often seen them covered with bees. A better solution is to coat the ports with Avon's *Skin-So-Soft*. Apply it lightly with a cotton swab. *Skin-So-Soft* is a very effective insects repellent and many people have found that is very effective.

### Q. How can I keep ants out of my hummingbird feeders?

**A.** A simple device called an ant guard effectively prevents ants from getting into feeders. It is simply a small moat-like saucer from which you hang the feeder. You fill the moat with salad oil and the ants get trapped in the liquid when they try to cross the moat. Ant guards are available from any wild bird supplier for just a few dollars. And some nectar feeds come with built-in any guards.

**Q. Do migrating hummingbirds ride piggyback on other birds?**

**A.** No. Hummingbirds fly under their own power. Some even make a 24-hour, nonstop 500-mile trip across the Gulf of Mexico.

**Q. When should I take my nectar feeders down in the fall?**

**A.** Contrary to popular belief, there is no reason to take hummingbird feeders down on Labor Day. Feeders do not tempt hummingbirds to stay north and die from the cold. Changing day-length, not food supply, dictates their schedule.

It is true that adult male hummers begin to head south in mid-August and that adult females and juveniles leave in late August and early September. But many hummingbirds that spent the summer farther north will trickle south well into October. Keep nectar feeders filled until you don't see a hummingbird for a week. That's usually mid-October for me.

## The "Hole" Story 12-5-91 (3/91)

Quiz time! What do bluebirds, chickadees, titmice, wrens and nuthatches have in common?

Here's a hint. Great-crested flycatchers, kestrels, screech-owls, wood ducks and purple martins share the characteristic, too.

If you answered that these birds are all cavity-nesters, give yourself a gold star. Unlike most birds, these build their nests in old woodpeckers holes, other natural tree cavities and nest boxes.

And because each of these birds uses nest boxes and is easy to observe, questions about their nesting biology often come up.

For example, are cavities, which would seem to be very secure places to nest, safer than open nest sites? Are cavity-nesters more successful than open-nesters? (Birds such as robins and cardinals, which build their nests in trees and shrubs, are called open-nesters.)    Why do so relatively few species nest in cavities?   Only about 85 of the 650 North American breeding birds use cavities. Here's the "hole" story.

It seems obvious that, compared to an open nest, a cavity should provide better protection from the elements and predators for both the nestlings and the incubating adult. Cavities are well protected from rain, and insulated from late spring freezes and mid-summer heat.   And only predators small enough to enter the hole or strong enough to tear apart the cavity pose a threat.

Furthermore, cowbirds, which   "parasitize" other birds' nests by laying their eggs in them,  rarely choose the nests of cavity-nesters.   They prefer to pick on warblers, vireos and sparrows.

Does this protection mean higher nest success?  Yes.  If measured as the percentage of nests that fledge at least one young bird, nest success is much higher in cavities than in open nests.  Nesting studies have shown that 60 to 80 percent of cavity nests succeed, while only  20 to 40 percent of open nests are successful.

But if cavities are such great places to nest, why don't all birds use them?  Simply because cavities are usually in short supply  --  there are usually more pairs of cavity-nesters than cavities.   This leads to fierce competition for  cavities and lots of time and energy  spent  defending nest sites.  That's  why it's so easy to get cavity-nesters to use nest boxes placed in suitable habitat.

Also, birds require certain physical skills and behaviors to use cavities.  Cavity-nesters must have strong feet that can cling to the face of a cavity.  And they must be curious and fearless about exploring dark holes and crevasses.  Virtually all cavity-nesters possess these traits.  Open-nesters do not.

Cavity nesters differ from open nesters in other ways, too. For example, they nest early in the season.

One incentive to nest early is to beat the post-winter emergence of black rat snakes.   Rat snakes are excellent climbers and routinely search tree cavities for food.    But when they first appear  in April, they tend to be sluggish and not terribly hungry.  By May, however,  they become a primary predator of cavity nestlings.   So if a bird can get a brood off before snakes get ravenous, it avoids a major predator.

Cavity-nesters also take advantage of the security cavities provide by extending the brood rearing period. Nestling bluebirds, chickadees and wrens, for example, remain in the nest for 16 to 22 days. Compare this to a nestling period of just 10 to 13 days for cardinals and robins. The extra time in the nest permits young cavity-nesters to leave the nest bigger, stronger and more able to fly than their open-nesting counterparts.

## Ghost Trees (1/95)

While visiting a wild bird specialty shop near Parkersburg, W.Va. a few years ago, the conversation turned to innovative ways to attract more backyard birds. When Kathy Cain, the owner of the store, mentioned "ghost trees," she caught my attention.

Ghost trees, Kathy explained, are simply dead trees. I call them snags. Kathy said she had one in her backyard. "In fact, it is the centerpiece of my feeding station," she proudly claimed. "I hang feeders from its branches, and the birds just love it."

I've been a long-time proponent of backyard snags, so I found Kathy's testimonial fascinating. The big drawback, of course, is that most neighbors frown on dead trees. "What did your neighbors say when they realized you weren't going to remove an obviously dead tree?" I asked.

"Most accepted the idea after we explained its purpose, but it didn't die," Kathy replied. "We planted it."

Now I knew I had found a kindred spirit. In 1981, I "planted" several small snags in my backyard in Stillwater, Oklahoma. I'm sure the neighbors are still talking about it. One assured me repeatedly that no matter how much I watered it, a dead tree wouldn't grow. But planting snags was the only way I knew to test their appeal to birds.

Back in the late 1970s wildlife biologists began to appreciate the importance of snags in natural ecosystems. Woodpeckers (primary cavity-nesters) excavate nest cavities in them and tear them apart in search of the insects that riddle their innards. In subsequent years tree swallows, bluebirds, titmice, wrens, screech-owls and kestrels (secondary cavity-nesters) nest in the old woodpecker holes. Deer mice, flying squirrels, tree frogs, arboreal snakes and lizards and myriad invertebrates also find shelter in abandoned cavities.

Red-tailed hawks perch on tall snags and scan the earth below for prey. Phoebes launch their fly-catching attacks from open branches on snags. Vultures roost on snags so they can bask in the early morning sun to warm their bodies. And many song birds -- indigo buntings, cardinals and bluebirds come immediately to mind -- sing from the tops of snags to advertise and defend their territories.

My fascination with snags and the birds they attract began in a meadow in southern Michigan in 1978. A single large snag in a brushy fencerow interrupted endless acres of corn and hay fields. One June morning I watched three species -- kestrels, house wrens and downy woodpeckers -- tending active nests. I've been hooked on snags and the "hole story" ever since.

Over a period of decades, a large dead tree teems with all manner of life until natural decay takes its final toll. Then the snag topples to its final resting place. There, fungi and other decomposers return the stuff that trees are made of -- organic matter and minerals -- to the soil, where it can be reincorporated into new trees. By planting snags in our backyards, we can observe this entire process of death, rebirth, decay and renewal.

At first, the idea of landscaping with dead trees seems laughable. But understanding snag ecology, especially its importance to birds, can turn an eyesore into a thing of beauty.

In winter, flocks of colorful birds visit snags that support entire feeding stations. In the spring, indigo buntings and cardinals sing from the highest branches. In the summer, hummingbirds mob the honeysuckle planted to embrace the towering skeleton. And in the fall, flocks of migrants perch and rest as they prepare for the long trip south.

## *Nest Box Basics* (1/88)

A basic nest box measures 4-inches-by-4-inches-by-10-inches high with an 1 1/2-inch entrance hole. This will do for bluebirds, chickadees, titmice, nuthatches, wrens and prothonotary warblers. Be sure to allow some way to open the box, so you can clean it after each nesting.

Use exterior plywood -- it's relatively cheap, it weathers well, and it has a nice rustic look. Any wood will do, however. Use 3/4-inch stock; it insulates nests from spring chills and summer heat.

Use rust-proof screws or galvanized nails to put the box together. This will increase the life of the box by several years.

The actual design and appearance of the box is unimportant to the birds. However, here are a few details to keep in mind.

Place the center of the entrance hole two inches from the top of the box. Keeping the hole as high as possible makes it more difficult for raccoons and cats to reach in and raid the nest. The best defence against predators is to mount a metal baffle below the nest box.

The roof should extend two or three inches beyond the front of the box to protect the entrance hole from driving rains. It may be flat or slanted. Drill four 1/4-inch drain holes in the floor so the box drains well after a heavy rain.

And NEVER put an outside perch on a bird house. Most cavity-nesting birds have very strong feet and can easily cling to any wood surface. A perch only encourages house sparrows, which are exotic, vicious pests.

House sparrows monopolize natural cavities and nest boxes and drive off native species, such as bluebirds and chickadees. Sometimes house sparrows actually drive these birds off their nests and kill the young before building their own nest on top of the first one.

If house sparrows are a problem, build a box that is only five or six inches deep and lower the front 1 3/16 inch to create a slot entrance. Bluebirds won't mind, but house sparrows don't like these modifications.

For more information about nest boxes and the birds that use them, refer to *A Guide to Bird Homes* (1995) by Scott Shalaway ($3.95 postpaid from Bird Watcher's Digest Press, P.O. Box 110, Marietta, OH 45750.)

## *50¢  Bluebirds*                                     (8/95)

How much is a bluebird worth?  Or put another way, how much does a bluebird cost?  These may seem  curious queries, but for those of us who monitor nest boxes, they are valid questions.  Economics -- costs and benefits -- plays a critical role in wildlife conservation.  This year I managed to put a price on the head of some cavity-nesting birds.

One of the reasons cavity-nesting birds use cavities is because they are relatively safe from predators.  As many as 80 percent of nests in cavities fledge at least one chick.  This compares to 20 to 40 percent for open nesters such as robins, cardinals and mourning doves.

Nest boxes, which are simply man-made cavities, are just as safe as natural cavities so bluebirds, chickadees, wrens and tree swallows often use them.  In nature there is a steady supply of new cavities, thanks to woodpeckers and decay. The annual supply of new cavities tends to be randomly distributed, so predators must constantly search for them. Nest boxes, on the other hand, last for many years and can always be found in the same place.  Predators, especially raccoons, eventually figure this out and return regularly to familiar nest boxes.  In this way, nest boxes often become predator feeders after just a few years.

Learning this lesson has taken years of field work and experience.  I finally questioned the wisdom of maintaining a trail of 50 progressively less successful nest boxes.  Maybe I ought to concentrate on fewer boxes and try to make them predator proof, I reasoned.  So this spring I invested $400 to create 10 predator-proof nest boxes.  I bought 10 treated, 4x4x8 ft. posts ($8 each), 10 heavy-duty predator baffles ($30 each) and I built 10 nest boxes at a cost of about $2 each.

I picked 10 locations that bluebirds or chickadees have used in the past, dug post holes and placed the baffles on the posts beneath the boxes.  Over the course of this nesting season the results have been phenomenal.  Bluebirds or chickadees used seven of the 10 predator-proof boxes.  One set of bluebird eggs never hatched, but the other six nests all fledged chicks.  Nest boxes have occupied these locations for nine years so older, experienced raccoons and rat snakes surely know their locations.  Yet predation dropped to zero.

The key to this success is the predator baffle. Many styles are commercially available, but many are cheap and flimsy. I chose those made by Erva Tool & Die Co. in Chicago. The baffle is a 28-inch long cylinder made of heavy sheet metal. The top has a round or square hole to accommodate either a 4x4 post or a round metal pipe. The seven-inch diameter cylinder prevents predators from climbing over the baffle; the closed top prevents them from climbing directly up the post. I selected Erva baffles because they are heavy and well made. I expect them to last at least 10 years.

All this sounds fine, you say, but isn't $400 a lot to invest in just 10 nest boxes? It certainly is -- if you simply look at it as a one time cost and benefit. But I see this as a long term investment. I estimate very conservatively that each unit will last at least 10 years. Immediately that reduces my cost to $40 per year or four dollars per box per year.

Furthermore if we assume that seven boxes will be used each year and that each used box will produce five chicks (a reasonable average), the annual cost of producing bluebirds and chickadees works out to $1.14 per individual. Finally, bluebirds usually nest at least twice each year, so the cost of producing bluebirds in boxes used twice each season drops to a bit more than 50 cents per bluebird. If birds use more than seven boxes and an occasional bluebird raises three broods, the per bird cost drops even more.

One of the most challenging problems in the business of conservation is attaching a price tag to wildlife. I'm no economist, but I think that's what I've just done. If bluebirds and chickadees cost between 50 cents and a dollar to produce, I'm willing to pay that price to insure they can nest safely and successfully on my property. In my mind, it's a bargain.

# *Backyard Water* (8/96)

When I was a graduate student, I lacked the time and money required to manage my small backyard. As I traveled back and forth to my study site each day, though, I noticed that quite a few homes had bird feeders and baths.

One hot August morning, after a thunderstorm had relieved a month-long drought, I noticed many birds gathered in a yard at one of the houses near my study site. I stopped and watched. Over the course of 30 minutes, robins, cardinals, doves, song sparrows, a catbird, a house wren and a downy woodpecker visited that yard. The lure was an old concrete bird bath that had filled with water during the early morning downpour.

As the birds came and went, I noticed a definite method to their routine. First they drank. Then they bathed. A few seemed to linger and soak.

I watched one cardinal intently. It bent its legs, then dipped down and submerged its body. As it emerged, it flapped its wings to help saturate its body. Then it hopped onto the edge of the bowl, fluffed its feathers and preened.

Reaching back to the base of the tail, it massaged a small gland with its bill. The gland released a dab of oil, which the cardinal then smeared over its feathers. The oil cleans, lubricates and waterproofs the feathers so they will last until the next time the bird molts.

Keeping feathers clean and healthy is routine maintenance -- without it, birds couldn't survive. Feathers protect the skin, minimize body weight, insulate and streamline the body, enable birds to fly and provide the colors that help birds recognize each other. A dependable supply of fresh water helps birds keep their feathers fit.

Water also helps birds meet some of their daily physiological needs. On hot days birds sometimes seem to soak in a bowl of fresh water just to cool off. Clean drinking water also enables birds to replace the water they lose by evaporation.

The simplest way to provide water is to put up a bird bath. It could be anything from an inverted garbage can lid on a tripod of rocks to a polypropylene saucer on a metal stand or even a small pond complete with pump and waterfall. You are limited only by your imagination and budget.

Regardless of how sophisticated you may choose to get, here are some tips to keep in mind:

• Keep the water no more than two inches deep. This is not a problem with most saucer-style baths, but if you install a small pool or pond, pile a stack of rocks to make one end shallow enough for small birds to bathe.

• Place the bath in open shade. It should be shaded between noon and 4 p.m. so the water doesn't get too hot. Overhead cover also provides safe haven when a cat or bird-eating hawk enters the area.

• Keep a bath at least 15 feet from any feeders. Seed hulls and droppings soil water rapidly.

• Change the water and rinse the bowl daily. A plastic scouring pad makes quick work of most grime. Algae, droppings and wind blown debris can turn a bird bath into a germ-infested "soup" in just a few days.

• Add a mister or a dripper. Birds find the sound of moving water irresistible. Dripper valves can regulate the flow of water from a steady stream to just a few drops per minute. Misters spray a fine mist of water above the bath, or they can be placed in a tree or shrub to simulate a refreshing summer rain. Warblers, vireos, hummingbirds, orioles and tanagers are just some of the neotropical migrants that enjoy bathing in a humid tropic-like mist.

If there's a magnet that will attract birds to your backyard all summer long, it's fresh water.

## *Winter Water* (1/91)

Orioles and scarlet tanagers in November? Thanks to unusually mild fall weather, I saw these two summer residents much later than expected last year.

But these birds weren't in their usual habitat -- I saw them from my office while I worked. They were drinking from a newly installed, heated bird bath. If not for the bath, I surely would have missed these stragglers because they don't come to feeders.

Winter water  attracts straggling migrants, woodpeckers, bluebirds,  screech-owls and other birds that usually don't visit backyard feeders.   Baths also attract regular feeder visitors as well.

People have been providing warm weather water for birds for decades.   Ceramic and concrete bird baths decorate lawns all across the country.   But these materials crack when ice forms, so most people store their baths  for the winter.

Now, thanks to inventive birders such as David Arvidson, unbreakable plastic bird baths and safe, reliable submersible water heaters give us a chance to offer water all year long.

Arvidson, of Zimmerman, Minnesota first put out water for birds about 10 year ago when his wife bought him a bath for his birthday.   He quickly found that conventional bath materials such as concrete and ceramic just didn't hold up to Minnesota winters.   So he developed a polypropylene saucer that does.

Arvidson reports , "I see more birds (numbers and species) at my baths in winter than I do in the summer.   I've seen as many as 15 birds at one time on my baths.  My winter 'bath list' includes cardinals, pine siskins, goldfinches, house finches, purple finches,  juncos , chickadees, red- and white-breasted nuthatches and three species of woodpeckers."

I've seen similar results in just the few months since I've had my winter bath.   In addition to orioles and tanagers, finches, chickadees, titmice, cardinals and mourning doves have visited my water supply.

Providing water is like providing food.  Birds can survive without it.  But if it's there, they use it.   It's too convenient to ignore.

Though birds bathe in baths in warm weather, they visit them just to drink in the winter.   They stay on the edge of the saucer and usually don't even get their feet wet.  They seem to know that if their feathers got wet, they would loose their insulating ability.

In winter a submersible,  thermostatically controlled water heater is the key .  If the bath runs dry or the weather warms up, the heater turns itself off.   Just be sure to use a heavy-duty, outdoor extension cord.

Bird bath heaters use the same  technology used to warm water for domestic livestock.  Submersibles can keep at least a small pool of water from freezing even during the coldest weather.

Arvidson offers three tips for those just testing the winter bath waters.

"Routine maintenance is critical. I rinse mine out every day and scrub it down every two to four days with detergent and bleach." Dirty water serves as a reservoir for disease organisms.

Arvidson suggests cleaning the heater, too. "If it gets encrusted with lime or other mineral deposits, it won't operate efficiently. I use a vinegar solution to remove these deposits."

Finally, he advises not to put baths under feeders. Seeds, hulls and droppings foul the water too quickly. Save yourself a lot of cleaning time just by keeping the bath a few feet away from feeders.

Heated baths cost between $70 and $100. For serious birders, a winter bath is worth the cost and effort.

But simpler, home-made winter baths work, too. Birds learn quickly to come to a supply of hot water in a dish, if it's offered at the same time every day. A large plastic flower pot saucer or garbage can lid anchored with a heavy flat rock works well.

A winter bath of any sort will brighten your yard with more and different birds. Just yesterday blue jays, cardinals, a red-bellied woodpecker and a Carolina wren used mine.

## *Wildflowers* (4/95)

Native flowers set the stage for the theater in the wild. As a source of food, nesting material and cover, wildflowers create a dramatic and scenic background for other watchable wildlife, particularly butterflies and hummingbirds. Yet as the scope of watchable wildlife expands to include more than just birds and butterflies, wildflowers are gradually making the transition from supporting cast member to superstar.

The best and most conspicuous evidence of wildflower popularity are the plots planted along highway median strips in recent years. Local gardens clubs, civic organizations and sometimes individual citizens donate funds to help highway departments defray the costs of growing wildflowers.

Establishing acres of wildflowers is expensive. It includes the cost of the seed, soil preparation and specialized planting equipment. But that expense is more than offset by the spectacular displays travelers enjoy. Splashes of color along otherwise boring four-lane highways sure make traveling more enjoyable.

Of course, wildflower can be planted on a much smaller scale. A wildflower garden brightens any backyard. Wildflowers attract hummingbirds and more butterflies than you'll ever be able to count. They provides months of aromatic, colorful, fresh-cut flowers. With just a little planning, a modest investment and a little work, a yard full of wildflowers provides enjoyment May through September, year after year.

The key to a successful wildflower garden is planning. A wildflower garden is a long-term project. Annuals complete their life cycle in one year, but shrubs, vines and most perennials take at least three years to produce flowers. Bearing this in mind, I've made wildflower "yardening" a life long project. Each year I plant new beds of annuals and buy or transplant a few new shrubs and perennials. In nine years I've slowly but surely turned a barren ridgetop lawn into a colorful garden that teems with butterflies and hummingbirds.

Before beginning a wildflower garden, it's important to understand wildflower life cycles. Some pack a lifetime of growth into just a few months, while others can live for decades.

Annuals complete their life cycle in just one growing season. They bloom only once, then die. But they naturally reseed the plot for the following year. Annuals such as zinnias and marigolds are great for dressing up a yard until longer lived plants establish themselves.

Biennials have a two-year life cycle. Growth the first year is usually limited to a small set of leaves near the soil surface. Stems grow and flowers and leaves form the second year.

Perennials devote most of their first year's energy to root growth. Look for them to bloom in their second or third year, and for many years thereafter. After a bed of perennials establishes itself, it provides years of low maintenance enjoyment.

Here's a list of wildflowers that grow easily in any sunny, well-drained backyard setting. You'll find these in many seed catalogs or at local garden centers. I've included common name, scientific name, flower color, type of plant (P-perennial, S-shrub, V-vine) and whether it attracts butterflies (b) or hummingbirds (h).

- Bee Balm (*Monarda didyma*), red, P, b, h
- Butterfly Milkweed (*Asclepias tuberosa*), orange, P, b, h
- Joe-Pye Weed (*Eupatorium purpureum*), light purple, P, b
- Purple Cone Flower (*Echinacea purpurea*), purple, P, b
- Blazing Star (*Liatris spicata*), lavender, P, b
- Asters (*Aster* spp.), white, blue, purple; P, b
- Butterfly Bush (*Buddleia davidii*), lavender, S, b
- Trumpet Honeysuckle (*Lonicera sempervirens*), orange; V, h
- Trumpetcreeper (*Campis radicans*), orange; V, h

If you are the impatient sort, design your wildflower garden around a foundation of perennials, shrubs and vines, but include some annuals for immediate results. Among the easiest annuals to grow are zinnias, marigolds, sunflowers and black-eyed Susans. These attract butterflies all summer long, and hummingbirds visit to pick off the inexhaustible supply of tiny insects that live within the flower heads.

An even better way to shortcut the time from planting to showcase is to buy mature perennials at a reliable nursery. This can get expensive, however, so your budget might dictate that you start from seed.

The secret to a successful wildflower garden grown from seed is site preparation. It requires some time and effort, but the results are worth the investment.

First, mow the vegetation on the plot as short as possible. Then till the plot to a depth of just an inch. To cultivate deeper invites undesirable weeds and grasses to invade the freshly tilled plot.

Water the plot to stimulate undesirable weed seeds to germinate. Let these weeds grow for a week or two, then apply a nonresidual herbicide such as *Roundup*. Reapply the herbicide in another week or so to insure a clean seed bed. (*Roundup* breaks down and does not remain in the soil, so it does not affect the germination of new seeds. It works only on growing plants.) After the wildflowers germinate, weed by hand.

The best time to plant wildflower seeds depends on soil temperature. Different plants have different temperatures at which they germinate best. The ground should be at least 55°F before sowing any seeds.

When planting seeds, mix one part seed with four parts fine damp sand, then hand-broadcast. The moist sand provides a substrate for seedling growth and helps retain moisture around the seed. In dry years, water lightly once a week.

It is also important to have realistic expectations. You'll be lucky if half the seeds you plant germinate. And remember, some wildflowers bloom the first year, while the perennials don't blossom until two or three years after planting.

Mow wildflower plots only after most of the flowers have gone to seed. This will insure a supply of annual and biennial species.

Establishing a wildflower garden is not an overnight project. It requires a lot of care and attention the first two years. But once rooted, a wildflower garden attracts hummingbirds and butterflies and becomes the most vibrant and colorful part of the yard.

For more information about wildflowers, contact the National Wildflower Research Center, 2600 FM 973 North, Austin, TX 78725-4201. Or visit your favorite garden center.

## *Attracting Butterflies* (6/94)

Like robins and earthworms or cedar waxwings and berries, butterflies and wildflowers complement each other. Wildflower nectar attracts butterflies; in return, butterflies help pollinate the flowers they visit. It's part of nature's balance.

The butterfly/wildflower partnership is one most homeowners welcome into their backyards. In fact, many folks plant wildflower gardens to attract butterflies. Sounds simple and obvious. Often, however, success is limited. People plant expensive gardens of nectar-producing wildflowers, but attract few butterflies.

The solution to this dilemma is understanding butterfly natural history. Their life cycle is described as "complete metamorphosis." Adults lay eggs, which hatch into caterpillars. After several week of growth, a caterpillar attaches itself to a piece of vegetation and forms a chrysalis. Inside the chrysalis, one of nature's most wondrous miracles takes place; the caterpillar transforms into a butterfly. The metamorphosis is complete.

The reason we see few butterflies, in spite of lavish butterfly gardens, is that too often we focus solely on the beautiful showy adults -- the butterflies. We must remember that in order to have butterflies, we must first have caterpillars. And often the plants caterpillars eat are not the same ones that produce their favorite nectars. To attract butterflies to the backyard, we must provide caterpillar food as well as nectar.

The rub is that caterpillar food plants are often weedy and less showy than the nectar-producers that make beautiful garden plants. Nettles, thistles, plantains, grasses, and variety of trees and shrubs are among the most important caterpillar foods.

With that background, here's how to attract butterflies to the backyard. Most butterflies prefer open, sunny locations so backyards are ideal -- if caterpillar food is available.

1. Mow less often, and mow a smaller portion of the yard.

2. Allow a patch of weeds to grow in a corner of the yard
If you live in an ecologically primitive community that enforces anti-weed ordinances, make sure your weed patch cannot be seen from the street. Many of the grasses and weeds that mature in these protected areas provide caterpillar food.

3. Reduce the use of herbicides and pesticides. People who routinely treat their yard with chemicals won't see butterflies. Herbicides kill caterpillar food plants, and pesticides can kill both caterpillars and adults.

4. If you have weed or insect problems, treat them individually. Spray chemicals directly on the offending pest

rather than treating the entire backyard. It seems silly to spend a lot of time and money cultivating beautiful flower gardens only to drive off butterflies with chemicals. A backyards isn't a golf course.

These few simple suggestions will save time and money and bring butterflies to your backyard. But remember, it's important to maintain a balance between nectar plants and caterpillar food plants. If you feed the caterpillars, but don't provide nectar, the adult butterflies will leave. Conversely, if you ignore the caterpillars, but plant lots of nectar-producers, you'll only see an occasional butterfly flutter by.

To give you a feel for who eats what, here's a list of some common butterflies and the plants their caterpillars eat: tiger swallowtail (yellow poplar, wild cherry), spicebush swallowtail (sassafras, spicebush), fritillaries (violets), question marks (nettles), mourning cloaks (willows, birch, elm), red admiral (nettles), painted lady (thistle), buckeye (snapdragons, plantains), monarch (milkweeds).

Adult butterflies are less selective about their nectar sources. Plant just a few of these wildflowers to turn your backyard into a nectar bar: bee balm, butterfly milkweed, butterfly bush, Joe-Pye-weed, lantana, marigolds, purple coneflower, zinnias. You'll also be delighted when you discover that hummingbirds use the nectar garden as much as the butterflies.

Get started this weekend. Visit your favorite garden center, and start with marigolds, zinnias, bee balm and butterfly milkweed. I promise your backyard will never be the same.

## For More Information:

Bat Conservation International
P.O. Box 162603
Austin, TX  78716

Hawk Mountain Sanctuary Association
RR 2, Box 191
Kempton, PA  19529

National Bird-Feeding Society
P.O. Box 23
Northbrook, IL  60065

National Wildflower Research Center
2600 FM 973 North
Austin, TX  78725

National Wildlife Federation
1400 16th St., NW
Washington, D.C.  20036-2266

The Nature Society
Purple Martin Junction
Griggsville, IL  62340

North American Bluebird Society
P.O. Box 6295
Silver Spring, MD  20906

North American Butterfly Association
4 Delaware Road
Morristown, NJ  07960

Project FeederWatch
Cornell Lab of Ornithology
P.O. Box 11
Ithaca, NY  14851

Purple Martin Conservation Association
Edinboro University of Pennsylvania
Edinboro, PA  16444